DATE DUE

GAYLORD   PRINTED IN U.S.A.

TWENTY-THREE KEYS TO INNER PEACE

TWENTY-THREE KEYS
TO INNER PEACE
from the Twenty-Third Psalm

A. E. Carpenter, B.A., Th.B., Th.M., Th.D.

Exposition Press　　*Hicksville, New York*

To:
Cecil, Alice, Richard and Alice Ann

First Edition

© 1974 by A. E. Carpenter

ISBN 0-682-48058-4

Printed in the United States of America

Contents

Preface

The past decade has been one marked by the lack of individual spiritual direction. Our church buildings stand as religious symbols for us Americans, but too often they are only mere street locations for our individual religious affiliations. We began this decade with a pill culture—pills to give us drive, pills to make us alert and more energetic, and pills to slow us down and put us to sleep at night. Bewildered adults have sought reassurance from their cocktail glasses while their children have sought it from narcotic trips into worlds of unreality. Somehow and somewhere the soul has lost its spiritual direction.

The average American today needs to regain his spiritual direction. Pious platitudes uttered in a raftered, vaulted cathedral, lighted with beautiful stained-glass windows, air-conditioned, and with cushioned seats for our comfort, no longer kindle a spiritual response from the average listening worshipper.

Theologians have never been more eloquent than today, but the words seem more meaningless to those to whom they are addressed. Millions of well-pointed sentences and properly entoned words are spoken each Sunday from our pulpits but seem so unrelated to the needs of a computer-oriented society. Modern man cannot feed his personal problems into a computer and get an answer for his spiritual needs. All of us wish it were that simple. The empty pews of the churches of the world are not a judgment of modern man, nor of religion itself, but of our methods of presenting religion to man. Something important is being lost in translation. These increasing numbers of empty pews should send out a tremor of great magnitude to be recorded on our religious Richter scale. This tremor should shake down many of the old theological walls of our seminaries. Their disappearance would hardly be noticed in this scientific age.

In desperation, man is turning to substitutes. This is particularly true of many of the youth all around the world. Our present age is like unto a picture painted of this age by an old-time prophet. He describes it as a man who cuts down a tree. This man uses most of the wood to cook himself a meal. After satisfying his physical needs for food, he feels a spiritual need unmet. What does he do? He uses a scrap of wood left over from the tree he felled and carves for himself a wooden image. He then falls down and worships the god he created by his own hand out of the scrap of wood. (Isa. 44:15-20).

I do not believe that the average American is living in revolt against God, nor does he accept the theory that God is dead. I believe the average American has simply lost his spiritual bearings—his spiritual directions—and is trying to find his way back to God without a compass.

We send this book out with a prayer that the reader might regain his spiritual direction if he has lost it, or that he might find the Man of Peace if he has never met Him.

A. E. Carpenter
Paradise Valley
Scottsdale, Arizona
1973

Human society is a deadly jungle for the emotional man. Man cannot escape from it—he must live in it. He cannot avoid it, nor hide from it, nor avoid the scars it will leave on his emotional nature.

Man needs help outside of himself—a trail-blazer he can follow, a defender, companion, and an ally he can rely upon. He cannot walk through life alone.

A. E. C.

Introduction
The Twenty-Three Keys of Peace

The National Wool Growers Magazine carried an article in its December, 1949, issue of an interview by James K. Wallace with a Nevada sheepherder by the name of Fernando D'Alfonso. I read this article when it appeared in the condensed version in the *Readers Digest* in its June, 1950, issue. The article has lived with me all these years, and this book grew out of my reflections on this article.

The picture portrayed by Mr. Wallace of this shepherd was one of a patriarch of his guild, who had received the secrets of his guild from his father who, in turn, had received them from his father, and so on back from father to son, beyond the birth of Christ. He was more than a caretaker of his sheep—he was their shepherd.

My attention was attracted to this article by the description of the old shepherd preparing for the night. The last thing he did before retiring was to quote the Twenty-Third Psalm in his native tongue. Later, when asked to explain this action, the shepherd said that the Twenty-Third Psalm was the creed of his guild, and that it was always repeated each night before retiring to remind the shepherd of his responsibilities toward his sheep.

This article sent the writer back to the Bible to restudy this great Psalm. I also saw a reflection of this Psalm in the tenth chapter of John's Gospel. These two companion scriptures—one

from the Old Testament and the other from the New Testament
—formed the background for this book.

For many years, I have done personal, professional, and
family counseling. I have dealt with people from every strata
of society. So often I found myself recommending to these
troubled individuals, the wisdom contained in these scriptures.
I have used the material found in this book in lectures, radio
and television broadcasts, as well as in face to face consultations.
Because of the enthusiastic acceptance of this material, I decided
to write this book.

What is Peace? It means many things to many people.
Surely, it is not merely a physical reaction of the body in response to the absence of pain. A healthy person can live in fear,
without pain, and still not have peace. It is not the absence of
negatives in our environment. Some of the most challenging
personalities this writer has ever known were persons living in
a hostile environment, or who lived in great physical pain.

What is Peace? Peace can be defined as a state of mind—of
the soul. There is no inner conflict or detraction that shatters the
state of peace. It lives above the mundane things of life. Real
peace of mind is the result of being lifted above the daily clouds
of fears, frustrations, and the uncertainties we face in our world.
Peace is never offered to us just for the giving. It is not a gift
you can give to another. You cannot go out into the world market
of emotions and say, "I want to buy peace." It is not for sale.
The harder you strive for peace, the more elusive it becomes.

What is Peace? It is a by-product. It comes as a crown—a
reward. Peace does have a price tag. Someone has paid a price
for your peace. Let me illustrate this from the Bible. In John
20:19-22, we have the account of Jesus meeting his disciples
as a group for the first time after his crucifixion and resurrection.
He appeared suddenly before them and said, "Peace be unto you
[Stop your fearing]; as my Father has sent me, even so send I
you," and when he had said this, he breathed on them and saith

unto them, "Receive ye the Holy Spirit." His peace came from Calvary!

Jesus found these early disciples hiding behind locked doors out of fear of those who had caused the death of Christ. They were enslaved by their fears and doubts. They had come to the end of three glorious years of walking with the Master, and what began as a magnificent dream had now ended in despair, as they sat in the locked room, still in shock, surrounded with their shattered dreams, hope gone, and with their empty lives. Life had suddenly ended for them. They had lost their sense of peace. Then Jesus appeared in the room and said to them these words, "My peace I give unto you." These words sent these men out to conquer and to die for His cause. But in their conquest, and in their death, they never lost their peace. It was a gift from God, Himself. This kind of peace kept them lifted above their environment and met their every need!

If you feel a need for peace of soul—and we all do—I believe you can find it within the pages of this book. Read one chapter, close the book, close your eyes, and silently meditate on the material you have read. Read a chapter a day for twenty-three days. I believe it will do wonders for you.

CHAPTER 1

The Key of a
Personal Relationship with God

There are two great shepherd scriptures in the Bible that should be read and studied together. One is this Twenty-Third Psalm in the Old Testament, and the other is the tenth chapter of John's Gospel in the New Testament. The latter is based upon the first. We will bring these two scriptures together in this series of thoughts.

The first key to inner peace of the soul as suggested by the Twenty-Third Psalm is, "Peace of heart comes from a simple, direct relationship between man and his God." Man cannot have spiritual peace without this. David, the shepherd, said in this Psalm, "The Lord is *my* shepherd." Jesus said, verse twenty-seven in the tenth chapter of John's Gospel, "My sheep hear my voice." The old Nevada sheepherder was more than a keeper of sheep. He was a shepherd of his sheep. His sheep knew that not only were they his sheep, but he was their shepherd. They roamed the hills together, slept together, drank out of the same streams together, and were constant companions day and night. Oh yes, the shepherd might be paid by a corporation in New York City, and the sheep owned by the same, but as far as the sheep were concerned, their shepherd was their owner. They belonged to him and he belonged to them. Their peace came from their personal, daily contact with this shepherd.

"The Lord is *my* shepherd." What simple, yet beautiful expressions—simple, personal, but oh, how wonderful! What significance this personal pronoun carries for us. This fact cannot be ignored. Man cannot have an abstract relationship with his God and find peace with God. Jesus knew this, so he said, "When you pray, say, 'Our Father which art in Heaven.'" Those two words—"Our Father"—did more to make God a personal friend to man than all the great miracles and expressions of God's power found in the Old Testament. They brought God out of the clouds of abstractions into a simple direct relationship with man, for man could understand the meaning of the word "Father." There was a tremendously close relationship between fathers and sons among the Hebrew families of the Old Testament—far closer than it is today.

There can be little satisfaction, or little peace for man, if he has an abstract relationship with his God. It is like falling in love with a statue. It matters not how much one might admire a beautiful statue, even if it is a reproduction of someone you love, and you might even learn to love it, but you cannot receive from it any love in response to your love. Abstractions might challenge the mind of man, as found in the field of physics, mathematics, and kindred other subjects, but they never can satisfy the longings of the soul, for the soul needs more than cold facts to warm and comfort it as it lives in a cold and selfish world. It needs a response from a responding God to give meaning to the facts he has learned about his God. "The Lord is my shepherd" is a cry of a happy and well-adjusted soul.

Many disturbed minds today result from abstract conceptions of God. God, to many people, and to a vast number of church members, is just a name with no more personal meaning to them than the planet Mars, or some distant and unseen star. This is why man turns to the visible things of life to satisfy the hunger of his soul. This is why so many are unhappy inwardly. The Lord is not their shepherd—the Lord is a stranger to their hearts and they really and honestly do not know Him at all in a personal way. He is not their "Father," but an impersonal God. Thus, they fear His wrath, His judgment, and His justice. Sheep have no fear of their shepherd. They know that he loves them and that they can trust his judgment. They lie down at night without fear because they know that their shepherd is near. They do not worry about the pasture for tomorrow for their shepherd did not fail them today.

You cannot have peace of heart unless you do enjoy a personal relationship with your God. Your soul is like the sheep of this Psalm; it needs to know that it has a shepherd it can see and feel at all times. It needs to know that it is loved, and can give love in return. It must say, "The Lord is my shepherd." Nothing less can give man the eternal peace of soul he needs to face this world of confusion, conflict, and unrest.

Not only will an impersonal or an abstract God fail to satisfy the demands of man's soul to meet life, but man cannot satisfy the cries of his soul for God by using "props" or substitutes for God because, in the end, these props either break down because they fail to fill man's need, or they become a God in themselves. This is why God so plainly said in the Bible, "Thou shalt have no other Gods before me. Thou shalt not make unto thee any graven image, or likeness of any thing that is in heaven above, or that is in the earth beneath, or that is in the water under the earth. Thou shalt not bow down thyself to them nor serve them; for I, the Lord thy God, am a jealous God, visiting the iniquity of the fathers upon the children unto the third and fourth generation of them that hate me, and showing mercy unto the thousands of them that love me, and keep my commandment." (Exod. 20:3-6). Nothing in the Bible is more plainly stated. It simply means that man is not to use any form of props, nor any physical substitutes in his worship of God. It means that a man who never attended church, nor had any personal contact with God, can not use the religion of his wife or children. So often I hear some man say, "I know that I ought to join the church, or attend church, but I send the children to Sunday School and my wife is faithful to her church and gives for us."

This satisfies no one. No, not even the person speaking. A wife cannot be a substitute for a husband before God. Peace of heart comes from a personal contact with God by each individual soul. No psychological escape mechanism can satisfy or take the place of "The Lord is my shepherd." Any prop placed between man and his God just removes him that much further from God. A picture of one's wife can never take the place of the wife herself. I spent three years overseas during World War II and I carried the pictures of my wife and two children with me wherever I went, and I looked at them often, but they were poor substitutes for the real persons, and they did not satisfy the longings of my heart for the real persons. Neither can any prop replace God in your soul.

God did not make man to be satisfied with anything less than a personal relationship with Himself. God cannot be satisfied with less than a personal relationship with man. "The Lord is my shepherd" satisfies both the shepherd and the sheep. God has to be real to you in a very personal way to give you the peace of soul you need. He has to be your shepherd. Any prop one might use to have fellowship with God only tends to push man farther away from God. Man does not have to approach God that way for we are invited to come boldly into his presence. Jesus said, "My sheep hear my voice." Not the voice of another speaking for me, or speaking to me. When you pray, do you really feel that you are talking to someone who is listening to what you are saying? And do you feel that you are talking to a real person? It ought to be that way with you, and it will be if you can say and mean "The Lord is my shepherd," and hear Jesus speaking, in return, through his words to us, "My sheep hear my voice."

There is still another thought in this one simple line, "The Lord is my Shepherd," and it is really the key to happiness for man—"The Lord is MY Shepherd." This is the personal pronoun and denotes ownership and a personal relationship. As far as each sheep was concerned, the shepherd was HIS personal and individual shepherd, and he was owned by the shepherd. The shepherd gave him individual attention all the time. Jesus says a strange thing in the twenty-eighth verse of the tenth chapter of John's Gospel: "My father, which gave them me, is greater than all; and no man is able to pluck them out of my father's hand." "My father gave them me." Did you get the meaning of this truth? God gives his Son, Christ Jesus, to me. I possess Christ as my very own as a gift from God. What could be more personal than that? And what could be more wonderful than that? This explains the verse ahead of this one, "And I give unto them eternal life and they shall never perish, neither shall any man pluck them out of my hand." You see, we are possessed by God and we possess Him. We can claim Him as our Father and Christ as our Saviour. Salvation is a two-way street for man. We give God ourselves and, in turn, Christ is given to us. What a difference it would make in our lives if we really believed this great truth—possessed of God, and possessor of God! Kept by the power of God, and living within the hand of God! The very thought should drive out fear, uncertainty, and plant a living quietness within our souls which could not be shaken by anything the world could throw at us.

This is illustrated by a story told by Dr. William L. Stidger in one of his books (*Sermon Nuggets*, page 12). He wrote, "A fire swept through the flimsy Negro quarters in a southern town and burned most of these homes. The next day, a white editor who was a personal friend to many of the Negroes went down to see a special friend, named Jim, whose house he learned had been burned to the ground with all of his earthly possessions. Not a thing was left. Much to his surprise, the editor found that, while most of the Negroes were wailing, lamenting and begging, Jim was smiling and full of good cheer, with a simple faith that all would come out right in the end.

"He talked with Him for a few minutes and then said, 'Well, Jim, this is what I call a real depression, conflagration and tragedy.'

" 'Mistah Jones, I dunno what all dem big words mean, but I been hearin dat fust one a lot lately. Dat one, what-chu-call-em "depression?" Dat what you mean dis am?'

" 'Yes, Jim, I would call this a real depression.' "

" 'Oh, no, I ain't got that, Mistah Jones. Hones' to God, I ain't got de real depression, cause, you see, I'se still got hope.' "

You see, what this wonderful Negro Christian was trying to tell the editor was that although he had lost everything he owned in that fire, he did not lose his God. He still had the foundation upon which to rebuild his life. His hope was still alive for his God and was a real and personal one to him. This is what Paul was saying in that great eighth chapter in Romans: "Nothing can separate us from the love of God which is in Christ Jesus, our Lord." (Rom. 8:39).

"The Lord is my shepherd." Do you want an abiding, satisfying peace in your soul? If you do, you will not find it outside of a personal, simple, direct relationship with God. Has it ever occurred to you that God made provisions for our needs before we had a need. He put oil into the ground before men invented the gas engine, the airplane, or a diesel. He put electrons into the world before man invented electric lights, air-conditioning machines, radios, or television. He put the atoms in the world before Einstein gave us his theories that made possible the use of atomic power. Either we do not know, or we must have forgotten, that God has the supply for our every need—even before these needs occur. "The Lord is my shepherd, I shall not want." "They know me and follow me." If you would have inner peace of soul, keep reminding yourself that you must exercise genuine faith and confidence in the leadership of God in your life. Let God be your personal shepherd and you shall not want.

God's Way

Thy way, not mine, O Lord!
  However dark it be;
Lead me by Thine own hand,
  Choose out the path for me.

Smooth let it be, or rough,
  It will be still the best;
Winding or straight it matters not,
  It leads me to Thy rest.

I dare not choose my lot,
  I would not, if I might;
Choose Thou for me, O God!
  So shall I walk aright.

The kingdom that I seek
  Is Thine; so let the way
That leads to it be Thine;
  Else I must surely stray.

Take Thou my cup, and it
  With joy or sorrow fill;
As best to thee may seem;
  Choose Thou my good or ill.

Not mine, not mine the choice
  In things or great or small;
Be Thou my guide, my strength,
  My wisdom, and my all.

—HORATIUS BONAR, *1808-1889*

Chapter 2

The Key of
Simple Faith in God

The number one killer today is not war, not heart disease, cancer, nor any one of the many physical diseases known to man. It is not something that we "catch" from another contaminated person, nor does it come from an unknown virus. The greatest killer of human beings today is the thing we call worry.

This killer has been with the human race since man first sinned in the Garden of Eden. In fact, worry was the first penalty Adam and Eve paid for their sin. They "hid themselves from God"—they were afraid of God—worried about what God would say and do to them. This "worry trickle" has grown into a river which has swept unnumbered millions to an untimely death.

In chapter one, we began this series of thoughts on the "Keys to Inner Peace" based upon the Twenty-Third Psalm. We suggested that you take each chapter as you would a dose of medicine. They will give you the peace of soul for which the heart yearns. In this message, we noticed that sheep must have a shepherd to be contented sheep . . . "The Lord is my Shepherd." There must be a simple, and yet very personal relationship between the sheep and their shepherd. Sheep must have a shepherd. Man must have a shepherd, also, to be happy. He must have someone to whom he can turn for strength, for he knows that he cannot face alone the problems of this life and the uncertainties of the life beyond the grave.

Not just any shepherd will do. He must have one with whom he can have a personal relationship. Any abstract God can never satisfy the spiritual longings of man's soul. He must have a God who is like the shepherd of the Twenty-Third Psalm—"The Lord is my shepherd." Like the one Jesus says God is "When you pray, say 'Our Father.' " A substitute for this kind of shepherd can never give our souls the peace they need. Man does not want to, nor should he use a "prop," or a "crutch" to reach his God, nor does he have to use one, for Jesus said that he came to show men the Father so that they might know Him and, thus, feel free to approach him as they would their earthly father. David walked hand in hand with his God, and to David, God was as real as the shepherd was to his sheep. "The Lord is my shepherd" is music to the soul of man. Music which will drive out worry, fears, and doubts from our lives; that is, if we really will let Him be our shepherd.

This Psalm suggests a second thing man needs for inner peace. "The Lord is my shepherd, I shall not want." Man must have confidence in the shepherd to supply all his needs if he is to enjoy soul peace. One must have a simple, genuine, and child-like faith in the leadership of the Shepherd for his life if one is to have inner peace. Jesus, speaking in the tenth chapter of John's Gospel said, "They know me and follow me." Jesus is saying two things here about the Christian. He knows Christ, and this Greek word suggests more than knowing the name of a person, but it means knowing the person in an intimate way. It is to know in such a way as to give your complete faith and trust in another . . . so, knowing Jesus in that manner, "they follow me" is a natural conclusion. There are three things we ought to know—need to know—if we are to accept this second suggestion from this Psalm for inner soul peace.

We need to know that there are other voices in the world that are not God's voice which call to us. We must learn to distinguish between the false voice and God's voice. There are other shepherds in the world trying to get us into their sheepfold. For some strange and unknown reason, or reasons, I have found many people willing to acknowledge the spirit of God in this world, but they refuse to believe that the spirit of the devil is as active in their lives as God's spirit. The Bible warns us to test the spirit that moves us whether it be of God or the devil. One sometimes hears church people justify something they have done by saying, "I was led of the spirit to do this or that." They are right, but one should ask, "Whose spirit?"

Jesus tells those gathered around Him in the verse quoted, that they do not follow Him for they are not His sheep, but that the ones who are His sheep do follow Him. One who follows Christ's spirit never is led into something that harms him, into something that hurts God and His kingdom, nor gives great hurt to innocent people. No shepherd who loves his sheep would lead his sheep into poisoned pastures, nor into swift running waters, nor into the caves of mountain lions. Would God do less for His children?

If we are to follow the voice of God—the Good Shepherd— we need to know something about this Shepherd. We need to read His book, the Bible. We need to visit His house to see how He lives and to learn of the things He loves. You can learn a lot about a person by visiting in his home. Just look at the pictures on the walls of his home, the books and magazines on the reading table, the games in the playroom, and you will get a good impression of the kind of person who lives in that house. You will not get a very good opinion of God by looking at the average church member, nor by the way he acts and talks. And yet, a lot of people do judge God by those who profess to be His followers. You will not learn much of the love of God by examining the love for others of the average church member. You will learn little of the will of God for your life by studying the will of God for another. But you will learn of God's will by going into God's library—the Bible—into God's house, His house of prayer and worship, and by turning aside each day in the privacy of your prayer room for a quiet talk with Him before you begin the day and again at night before the day is over. The sheep follow their shepherd by being where he is. They keep their eyes and their ears atuned to his presence. They do not spend their time standing in the shade looking at him, nor listening to him as he sings or plays his flute. But they carry on their daily routine of eating, drinking, and resting within the sound of his voice and within the felt influence of his personal presence. And they have peace. They know his voice and they will not follow the voice of the stranger.

If you want to be sure you are following the Good Shepherd, perform to the best of your ability each day that which He gives you to do that day, and do not worry about how you are going to do the most difficult tasks tomorrow. Ask God for His daily leadership—then follow His direction. If you seek His will for your life each day, you will find it, for He says, "My sheep hear my voice; they know me and follow me." There is nothing mysterious about this. I knew the wishes of my parents for my life when I was a boy. I knew how I was expected to act in school, in church, and on the playground. I know what God expects of me in the same way. I admit, I sometimes learned the "hard way" of mother's will for me under certain situations, for mother was of the school that believed in not sparing the rod. But then, the rod was not applied because I did not know mother's will for me, but because I was not willing to follow it.

We do not have to play "hide and seek" with God to know His will. When we have met the first condition for inner peace —that of having a personal relationship with God through Christ Jesus, His Son—we can ask Him in a simple and direct way for His will for our life. He will reveal it to us. The trouble with most of us is, we are like the little boy who did not want to come home when his mother called him to supper. He had promised that he would come just as soon as he heard her call. When questioned by her later as to why he did not come when she called him to come home, he replied, "I kept my word, but mother, I played far enough away from home so that I would not hear you when you called." We just go on blundering through life without the will of God being known to us because we do not seek it, or because we are afraid of it, or because we do not want it. The happy sheep is the one that is feeding where the shepherd wants him to feed. He finds happiness in his simple faith in his shepherd.

Sheep know a second thing about their shepherd and this has given them the faith they need in him to supply inner peace for them. Sheep are creatures of learned habits—conditioned reflexes —and so are men. Sheep face their uncertain future in light of their past experiences with their shepherd. He has never failed them, nor has he ever forsaken them in the presence of danger, nor failed to meet their needs. I know some very fine Christians who live in the fear of another depression, and this robs them of the joy of their present abundance. They worry about values of tomorrow and are disturbed by every shifting economical wind. They cannot enjoy the blessings of God and of their country for they see fearful ghosts in the clouds of tomorrow. This is true to some degree in the lives of us all. What is wrong with us when we allow ourselves to drift into this frame of mind? And what can we do about it?

We need to review our past experiences with God—with our Good Shepherd—whenever we face unknown experiences. Ask yourself two questions. Has God ever failed to keep His promises in the past? Can you honestly say, "I failed because God failed me?" Do you know of any Christian who can point a finger in God's face and say to Him, "You have failed me?" Until you can do this, why doubt God in the future. But you say, "I don't doubt God, I doubt myself." To doubt yourself to meet any situation in life is to doubt God. He has said that He is our shepherd. He has said that He loved His sheep. He has said that a good shepherd would lay down his life for his sheep. He has said that He would never leave us nor forsake us. He also reminds us through the writings of Paul that if God is for us, who could be against us?

If our lives are filled with fears it is because we are living outside of the sheltering arms of His many glorious promises—we are outside of his sheepfold. Inner peace comes to any Christian who exercises a genuine faith in the leadership of Christ for his life. It is when we fail to do this that we fall victim to worry, and become a captive to our fears and doubts. A sheep eats in the pasture where the shepherd has brought it that morning. He does not worry about the pastures of tomorrow for he has faith in his shepherd to supply them for him. You can have strengthening, abiding soul peace to meet any difficult situation you might have to face if you look at the situation in the light of similar experiences with God in the past. If the Good Shepherd was adequate then, is there any reason to doubt His ability to handle the present or future?

Sheep have learned a third thing about their shepherd and, knowing this, they can nibble their grass during the day, and at night lay down and digest their food without fear of ulcers, for you see, they have learned that it was the job of the shepherd to supply all their needs. If they need water, the shepherd already has anticipated this need and he knows where to lead them to cool and refreshing water. When the sun rises to noonday heat, cool valleys are within reach, and when the grass in one valley is exhausted, the shepherd has already located another. What an important lesson for us to learn: God will supply our every need. I do not mean that the Good Shepherd will eat the grass for his sheep. He cannot do that for his sheep. He can only lead the way to where the grass is green, but the sheep have to eat for themselves, or starve.

God does not promise to feed and care for the lazy person, nor to provide shelter or clothing for a man just because he is a human being. God gives us the strength and the means with which to feed ourselves if we will use our strength. Jesus said that if God cared for the lily, the birds of the air, would He not do even more for His own? He then said, "O ye of little faith."

There is a challenging verse of scripture in the Thirty-Seventh Psalm, the twenty-fifth verse, "I have been young and now I am old; yet have I not seen the righteous forsaken, nor his seed begging bread." Have you? Listen to the words of St. Paul, "My God shall supply all my needs." (Phil. 4:19). "The Lord is my shepherd, I shall not want . . ." It is God's job to take care of His sheep—this is not the job of the sheep.

During a visit to Louisiana, one of my best friends said to me, "The longing of my heart is to have peace with God and to be a Christian. I have tried to find my way to God but cannot." He attended church that night where I delivered the message, but still did not find this peace he wanted. Then I suggested to him that he return home, get his wife out of bed, and kneel together beside their bed, hand in hand, and ask God for soul peace. The next night he said to me, "I did what you suggested, and during our prayer, a quiet peace came into my heart, and I am no longer afraid of the future. I do not know what happened, but I feel different now." This businessman now could say, "The Lord is my shepherd." What a difference it made in his life. Can you say this? Do you want to say this? Take Christ into your life as your Shepherd for He wants to be.

CHAPTER 3

Let Another Do Your Worrying—
God Is Willing

In the first two chapters on the Twenty-Third Psalm, we have already noticed two vital keys that will help unlock the inner chambers of the soul and give man peace. In the words of David, the great shepherd, "The Lord is my shepherd," we noticed that it is the close, personal relationship which exists between the shepherd and his sheep that produces calmness and confidence in the sheep. Each sheep knows his shepherd in a very personal way, and in turn, the shepherd knows each sheep in a like manner.

God made man in the beginning so that man could know God in a personal way and that God might also have somewhat the same relationship toward us as the shepherd has toward his sheep. When David penned the line, "The Lord is my shepherd," he was thinking of the wonderful relationship which he had with his God. Man cannot be happy within his soul without a similar relationship with God, for God made man with this desire to have such a relationship. God never plants a need within a man without also providing a source through which man may satisfy that need. He gave birds the instinct to fly, but he also gave them wings with which to fly. He gave fish an instinct to swim, but he also gave them the mechanics by which they could swim. God would do no less for His highest order of creation—man. If God gave man the desire to have a personal relationship with Himself (and He did), He also gave man the means and ways of obtaining it.

Christ came, saying, "I come to show men the Father, and if you have seen me, you have seen the Father. Knowing me is to know my Heavenly Father." "When you pray, say 'Our Father which art in Heaven.'" Paul was not boasting, but was stating a positive fact when he said, "I know whom I have believed . . ." This word "know" in the Greek language means to know in a very personal way—not a friendship by correspondence, or through some mutual friend, or one through some public publication, but it means to know in person—an exchange of personality attributes with another. When man knows God as "My Shepherd"—it does something to him. He finds soul peace.

The second key to soul peace which is to be found in this Twenty-Third Psalm is in the verse, "I shall not want." Sheep have simple faith, and yet, great faith in their shepherd. If he were to lead them over a cliff, they would follow. This faith is not theirs by birth, but by experience. Their shepherd has never failed them. To them he is the only shepherd in the world. They see other flocks of sheep and other shepherds, but voices of other shepherds they will not follow. Man becomes confused today by the many voices crying out to him. Peace is found when man listens only to the voice of God. "The Lord is my shepherd, I shall not want." "They know me, and they follow me." They follow their shepherd because of their simple and complete faith in him. Thus, they have peace. Man must have complete faith in God to be completely happy!

We come now to the third key of inner soul peace to be found in this Twenty-Third Psalm. "I shall not want." The sheep have found peace and are contented because they have learned to accept the diet provided daily for them by their shepherd.

It is the job of the shepherd to supply all the needs of his sheep. He makes the choice where they will drink. He tests the safety of the water by drinking it himself before the sheep are led down into it for water. He supplies their daily pastures. He must judge whether the grass is too scarce for grazing or if it is too short or too tough for the tender mouths of the lambs. He must provide shelter for them against the storms, against the dangers of the night, and against the heat of the noonday. Sheep are the most helpless of all domesticated animals. They must be shepherded or they die. Men are like sheep. They, too, need a shepherd—God.

Jesus illustrates this fact to the crowds one day by telling the story about the lost sheep. Why did the shepherd leave the other ninety-nine safe in the sheepfold, close the one opening so nothing could get in or none get out, and go into the stormy night to find the one sheep? Could not the sheep find its way back to the other sheep? Could it not take care of itself until it worked itself back to the flock? Was there not enough food for it to live upon until it found its way home? These things might be true of other animals, but not true of sheep. It would die alone in the midst of plenty without knowing plenty was near. So Jesus pictures the good shepherd going out into the night and searching until the lost sheep was found and then bringing the lost sheep home on his shoulders, rejoicing over the fact that he had found it alive.

Man needs the Good Shepherd, for man can die in the midst of plenty. All men hunger for God and for things of God. They cannot find the food to satisfy their hunger by themselves. They need a shepherd. Remember one of the beatitudes, "Blessed [happy] are those who hunger and thirst after righteousness, for they shall be fed—shall be satisfied." "The Lord is my shepherd, I shall not want."

Not only does God supply all our spiritual needs, but He also promises to supply all our needs. Paul, the great Apostle, once said that he was happy in whatever state he found himself because Christ Jesus supplied all his needs.

The last great depression is still etched in my memory. But not once can I recall a single case of any of God's children in great need—at least I did not know of any in our church. Have you ever heard of a Christian in America dying from starvation? You will not, if he will eat what God gives him. "The Lord is my shepherd, I shall not want."

Jesus says in the thirty-fourth verse of the sixth chapter of Matthew, "Take, therefore, no thought for tomorrow, for tomorrow shall take thought for the things of itself. Sufficient unto the day is the evil thereof." Mental hospitals are filled with people who were put there because of worry over things of tomorrow. They did not learn that the Lord wanted to be their shepherd, and that if He were, they would not want—for the Good Shepherd provides for every sheep.

When God becomes our Heavenly Father—when we place our faith in His Son, Christ Jesus—He becomes our shepherd in a very real sense. He will supply our spiritual needs, and He will also supply our physical needs. Did not Jesus say that since God took care of the lilies of the field, the birds of the air, that we could trust Him to take care of His children who are more precious to Him than common lilies and birds? "O, Ye, of little faith." To worry over material things is to doubt the word of God. Now God does not say *how* He will supply our needs, but He does say that He will supply them, in His own way.

I remember my father telling of an experience of a widow who had great faith in God to supply her every need. She was praying one day for food and she was overheard by some mischievous boys. They decided to have some fun at her expense. So they went to the store and bought her a basket of groceries and put the basket on her doorstep, rang the bell, then watched her reaction from around the corner of the house. They saw her go in the house, and when they peeked in the window, saw her fall to her knees, thanking God for His gift of food and for answering her prayers. Then they knocked on her door and told her that it was not God who had answered her prayers, but that they were the ones who had brought the food and that God did not have anything to do with it. She replied, "Oh, yes, God did send these groceries. He just used you for His delivery boys."

A second thing that every child of God needs to know about this text—"The Lord is my shepherd, I shall not want"—is THAT WORLD STANDARDS FOR OUR NEEDS ARE NOT ALWAYS GOD'S STANDARDS. God wants to give to all His children the pluses of life, but He cannot, and does not, until we learn to use wisely the basic needs of life. The love of God for us—for each of us—prevents Him from giving us the things that would spoil our lives for ourselves, others, and His kingdom.

Many times we seek things we ought not to have, and so entreat God for them that He gives them to us even though He knows they are harmful to us, so that He can teach us lessons we could not have learned otherwise.

Every parent should read Dale Evans' little book *Angel Unaware*. In this book she wrote about the lingering illness and death of her child. She and her husband, Roy Rogers, learned to walk with God, hand in hand, through this experience, and it changed their lives. God gave these two parents the grace to see beyond a tiny grave to the glories of a surrendered life. These fine movie stars have been the idols of millions of children around the world, and they have blessed millions of lives since this experience.

Ofttimes we say to God, "Give me ice cream and cake," but he gives us bread and milk instead. We ask him for a big salary and prestige in our jobs, but he gives us instead a job with little worldly prestige, and a small salary. We rebel against this when we see others getting ahead of us. Little do we know of the hardships and the price others pay to get what they have, and if we did know, it would make us satisfied with what we have. God knows the kind of diet we need. He knows what would make us happy and what would destroy us.

Man lives and dies within the framework of human values. We measure success by the other man's bank account, the size of his house, and the length of his car. We measure our success or failure by the kind of job held by other people. This is true even in the realm of religion. Preachers are judged by the size of their church, their salary, and the budget of their church. It is so easy to forget that God's diet is not the diet of the world, nor is the world's diet the same as God's. When the Psalmist David said, "The Lord is my shepherd, I shall not want," he was not thinking of the banquet table of the kings of Israel, nor did he have the slightest idea that someday he would be eating at such a table. He was thinking of the sheep before him, grazing on the lush green grass. He thought of the seasons—the lean and the fat—the abundance of grass and the scarcity of it, and he thought of the times they had to walk many miles to find water and a few blades of grass. He knew, too, that his sheep wanted to eat other things that looked good to them, and, no doubt, if they could have spoken his language they would have said, "Why do we have to eat half-burned-up grass when we see juicy green plants you have uprooted and placed out of our reach before you led us into this pasture?" They did not know that these plants contained poison and meant death to them, even though other animals might eat them without harm. David learned from the sheep to accept God's diet of our Great Shepherd. It comes when we learn to depend upon the Good Shepherd to furnish us with the kind of food we need. The one thought often overlooked is that which is known as the "Lord's Prayer"—the one that says, "Give us this day our daily bread." Now this does not mean we are asking for bread that day. If this were true, this portion of prayer would be a mockery for millions, for the bread they are to eat is already on the table or in their deep freeze. What it really means is, "Give us this day the kind of bread I ought to eat. Give me wisdom to choose the kind of food my body needs. Give me the strength to earn the money to buy the kind of food my body ought to have to live life at its best." Everyone needs to pray this kind of prayer—rich or poor alike. Learn to accept God's diet for your life, and you will have peace of soul.

God is concerned as much over the physical needs of his children as He is of their spiritual needs. One cannot be separated from the other. It is almost impossible to make a person who is starving believe that God loves him. Feed him first, give him a bath and a change of clothes, and then when he asks you "Why?" you can tell him of God's love for him as expressed through your own life.

God is spirit, and we are human beings, but we know that God cares for our bodies for much emphasis is given to the physical needs of the human race. God fed the five thousand before he spoke to them. He healed the ten lepers before saving one of them. And He performed many miracles for man. God does care for his children. A good shepherd never neglects, nor forsakes, his sheep—neither will God.

I saw a blind man the other day walking down the street. He came to a corner. His seeing-eye dog paused, looked in all directions, then guided his master safely across the street. He can safely guide his master anywhere in the city. But the dog was not all of the picture; you see, the blind man must trust the dog without question. He must follow the dog's directions. If man can place such complete faith and trust in a dog, why can't he trust God? Can you say and mean, "The Lord is my shepherd, I shall not want"?

> God knows the way of the righteous,
>   Even though it be dark and drear;
> He knows when we're tired and weary,
>   Our burdens too heavy to bear.
> We ask as the shadows lengthen,
>   "Lord, lift Thou this burden of care,"

And often His voice replieth:
  "My child, I placed it for you there,
With grace that is all sufficient,
  That you might grow stronger in Me,
So trust, weary child, your Father,
  He knoweth and careth for thee."
                              —*Gospel Herald*

CHAPTER 4

The Key of Assimilation

When I was a small boy, I discovered a strange fact. When I was out alone at night and became frightened, I seemed to be able to run like the wind. When I grew older, I read articles about how men performed great feats of strength when possessed with fear. I recall a fire in our neighborhood where a woman picked up a trunk and threw it out of the burning house. Later she found that she could hardly move it. Scientists tell us that there are certain glands in our bodies that release extra energy into our systems under stressed conditions. These glands come to our rescue in an emergency. They also tell us that if these glands are called upon too often to produce this extra burst of energy, they can produce heart disease and even cancer. Our bodies were not created to work at top speed all the time. Man often is not aware that he is calling upon his body for the extras of life too often until his health is broken.

The author of the Twenty-Third Psalm learned from God many valuable lessons about life. Just to quietly read it will relax your mind. And if one can really enter into the spirit of this wonderful little piece of sacred literature, he can gain what so many seek, yet so few find—inner soul peace. In the three previous chapters, we have considered three keys to inner soul peace. We find a fourth key in the next verse "He maketh me to lie down in green pastures." Man has to relax at certain intervals to keep spiritual and physical health. He has to learn how to live in the green valleys of life.

To this text from the Twenty-Third Psalm, add these other shepherd verses from the tenth chapter of John, and you will find another key to happiness: "I am the door; by me if any man enter in he shall be saved and shall go in and out and find pasture . . . I am the good shepherd . . . I am come that men might have life and that they might have it more abundantly . . . I am the good shepherd . . . He maketh me to lie down in green pastures." All these scripture verses are just one wonderful thought— the key of assimilation. A time for the soul of man to recover its lost energy.

The sheep of David's day would start grazing around 3:30 in the morning and would graze until about 10:00 A.M. The shepherd would plan grazing for the day so that the sheep would start eating rough grass early in the morning. The shepherd would schedule the sheep to arrive in an area of soft and tender grass around 10:00 A.M. The sheep would then lie down in the soft green grass and rest through the heat of the day. I remind you again that David was thinking about his personal relationship with God. He saw himself as the sheep, and God as the shepherd, caring for the sheep.

The Bible tells us that God is not a God of confusion nor disorder. God does not want his children to be either. Let us learn from David three lessons on how to relax and be happy as we travel through the Green Valleys of Life.

Sheep must be fed to be healthy and happy: "He maketh me to lie down in green pastures . . . I am the door; by me if any man enter in, he shall be saved and shall go in and out and find pasture . . . I have come that men might have life and that they might have it more abundantly . . . I am the good shepherd." These things are known to all sheepherders. Sheep feed best in flocks, never alone. You will find that animals such as lions, tigers, etc., who are destroyers and who feed upon other animals, feed alone. Even when the pack-type killers of the north make a kill, they do not like to eat with another and will kill each other to protect their privacy. Sheep eat best and are healthiest when they feed together.

Why did Jesus establish the church on earth? Christ did not say, "Each of you worship God in your own way beneath the stars at night, or in the forest or on the plains," but he did point out by practice and precept the importance of community worship. The very word for church suggests this idea. The word church comes from two Greek words "ek-klisia." The verb "klisia" means to call, and the preposition "ek" means out—to "call out" of the world. Therefore, we can say the word "church" means those who have been called out by God's spirit from the world and who have gathered themselves together in his spirit to commune with Him in songs, prayer, and study of His Holy Word.

No man can be spiritually healthy and neglect feeding with the flock. What is a worship service on Sunday? It can be called the flock of God feeding together. You cannot go into one of God's houses of worship seeking to be fed by God and not come away without receiving something. Oh yes, I know that many people go to church and come away still hungry, and they are quick to blame the minister, the music, and others for this failure to be fed, but never themselves. Suppose you would go to the dinner table today with a closed mouth. And as others around you passed the food to you, your mind was on something a thousand miles away, so preoccupied that you did not see what was being passed before your eyes. You might sit through the meal with your mouth closed, get up from the table, and say with all honesty, "I am still hungry." Too many people approach worship in the same manner. Often we approach church worship with the attitude, "I just dare you, Preacher, to feed me. I just dare you to stir my heart." And we sit back with a closed mind; bodies in church but our heart and mind elsewhere.

I once read the reply of a very learned man to these questions: What can you get out of church attendance? You are so far ahead of your pastor in your mental capacity, how can you get anything from his messages? Do you really go to church every Sunday? And do you get much from the services? He said something like this: "Church attendance is one of the most enriching experiences of my life. I go every Sunday because of the spiritual food I get. It is true that my minister is limited in his educational background, but he is a man of God. When his sermon becomes dull, I fix my mind upon some great truth he has mentioned, or I recall a text from God's word and meditate upon it. Thus, my soul is fed each Sunday. I love to be with God's people, and I do get something at my church on Sunday I cannot get elsewhere. Sheep feed best in a flock. Man worships best with other men." "He maketh me to lie down in green pastures . . . I am the good shepherd . . . they shall go in and out and find pasture."

With this idea comes a second important fact. Sheep, trying to feed outside the flock, become easy prey to the pack of wolves or other predators lurking just beyond the watchful eyes of the shepherd. Sheep are never attacked while feeding under the watchful care of the shepherd, and if such an attack is made, the shepherd would have to be destroyed before the sheep could be touched.

Satan has little opportunity to hurt the Christian who is feeding with the flock of God, but he is ever alert to those sheep who leave the flock to feed by themselves. They are the church members who become unhappy in their Christian experiences. They are the ones who become easy prey to new and strange doctrines, and they are the ones who get hurt in the end.

The church is to the Christian what rails are to a train. It is our margin of safety. When a train leaves its tracks, it is headed for trouble, and often for a great disaster. Of course the rails upon which a train travels are narrow, but their narrowness is their safety. Did not Jesus say "Narrow is the way that leadeth to eternal life, but broad is the way that leadeth to destruction." Sheep must live and graze within the bounds of the shepherd's personal vision. They have learned their safety rests within the vision of the shepherd.

Parents should realize the importance of rearing their children within the flock of God. An impartial study of the court records of any city in America will convince anyone who is honest with himself that Sunday School and church are the best things that can come into the lives of children. One of the last things Jesus said to his disciples was when he turned to Peter and said, "Feed my lambs." Well-fed lambs make good sheep. Undernourished lambs die young.

Look around you at the people you know. Ask this question of the ones who are the most unhappy and get so little from life: "Are you a member of a church and do you take an active part in the life of your church?" But find the happiest and best-adjusted person you know and ask that individual the same question. The latter will answer in the affirmative and the former in the negative. One cannot have soul peace and not feed with the flock. So often we hear it said, "The church needs men." This is not true. Men need the church far more than the church needs them. This is like saying to the shepherd of a flock, "The grass needs your sheep." No, the sheep must have the grass or they perish.

"He maketh me to lie down in green pastures . . . if any man enter in he shall go in and out and find pasture . . . I am the good shepherd." All this suggests a third characteristic of sheep. A sheep must be healthy in order to be happy, and to be healthy he must eat. No one can eat his grass for him. He must do his own grazing. The shepherd can and will stand guard while he eats, and the shepherd will find water for him, but no matter how much the shepherd loves his sheep, he cannot eat their food, nor drink their water. Now this is an obvious fact—so obvious that you say, "So what. Everybody knows this." "The Lord is my shepherd, I shall not want. He maketh me to lie down in green pastures." That which is obvious so often becomes obscure to us when we attempt to carry it over into our own lives. I repeat, David was not magnifying his sheep, but his God. He was thinking of his relationship with his God and trying to explain this relationship in words that would have meaning to men, not only in his generation, but for men in all generations. God had led David day by day. He had carried him into green pastures, to the still waters of life, and not once had David lacked for that which he needed. God had led him, but David ate for himself. Even God cannot eat for man.

God did not take the shepherd boy, David, and make him a great king of Israel overnight. God led him first into the valley of the kings before he ascended the throne. David ate that which God placed before him. David did not kill Goliath with a miracle, but killed him in thought a thousand times on the Judean hillsides as he practiced with his sling, and later protected his sheep by the skill he had acquired with that sling. David's great victories were not miracles of God, but were victories born of preparation, as David learned the arts of war as a young man fleeing for his life before King Saul. He had learned the terrain over which he fought his great battles years later as he led his sheep over every yard of it. He ate well in God's green valleys, ate at God's training tables. Football games are not won on Saturdays, but on the practice fields before Saturdays. Championships are lost or won in training. I do not think that God chose David just because there was a boy called David, son of Jessie, but God made a choice of David based on His foreknowledge of how David would accept his training.

Most of us want to be great Christians without eating the food that builds spiritual giants. We want to jump from the cradle into manhood without following the normal laws of growth. We forget that Christ himself had to travel the road of all men. Of the years he lived on this earth, thirty years were spent in preparation for the last three. Even the Son of God had to eat for himself.

I am grateful for two wonderful and saintly parents. Both were spiritual giants in God's kingdom. The Bible in our home was as familiar to us as the daily newspaper, and was read as often. Prayer was as much a part of our home life as our daily conversation with each other. Dad and mother did not do our Bible reading for us, nor our praying for us. They did not do our church attending for us, neither did we do theirs for them. They put the food before us and did teach us how to eat it, but we had to do the eating.

I entered college to become an electrical engineer. The Lord called me into His service during my second year of college. Later, when I entered the seminary, I was astonished at the great amount of Bible knowledge that had become a part of my life. I did not have to change any of my theology in the seminary, for as I walked through the green valleys my parents had taken me as a child, I had been taught to eat for myself. And having done so, that which I believed became my own. Sheep must eat for themselves; no one can eat their food for them.

One can never find peace of soul vicariously, nor can he get it through the medium of a friend, or a loved one. It comes to you only through a personal experience between you and God. This is what David meant when he said, "The Lord is my shepherd, I shall not want. He maketh me to lie down in green pastures." And what Jesus meant when he said, "I have come that men might have life and that they might have it more abundantly."

The Secret

I met God in the morning,
    When the day was at its best,
And His presence came like sunshine,
    Like a glory in my breast.
All day long the Presence lingered,
    All day long He stayed with me,
And we sailed in perfect calmness,
    O'er a very troubled sea.

Other ships were blown and battered,
   Other ships were sore distressed,
But the winds that seemed to drive them,
   Brought to us a peace and rest.
When I thought of other mornings,
   With a keen remorse of mind,
When I too had loosed the moorings
   With the Presence left behind.
So I think I know the Secret
   Learned from many a troubled way,
You must meet Him in the morning,
   If you want Him through the day.

CHAPTER 5

The Key of Relaxation

The most wonderful thing that God ever created was not the beautiful heavens above, the mysteries of the sea, nor the great mountains of the world with their eternal caps of snow and ice. The most wonderful thing God ever created was man, himself. From the top of his head to the bottom of his feet, man is a marvel. Man has studied the human body and mind since the day God made Eve from the rib of Adam, and man is still learning new things about the human body. Only God could have created a marvel like man.

Man was made to withstand things that destroy other animals. He can adjust to the heat of the tropics or the ice of the far North. He has learned to live on little food or much food. He has learned to live in space and to walk on the moon. He has learned to conquer everything on this earth except himself. He is possessed with a thing called a mind, which gives him a will and a choice. He can think and reason and thus liberate himself from habits that would destroy or from environments that would wipe out the human race. Man is a delicate machine with a soul. He is both a physical being and a spiritual being. There must be a proper balance between the two, or one will destroy the other in the end without profit to either.

Man has sought proper balance for his soul and body from the fields of Art, Science, and Philosophy, but regardless of where he searches he will not find it summed up so neatly and correctly as in the Twenty-Third Psalm. Take this Psalm and add to it the tenth chapter of John's Gospel, and one has everything he needs, not only to find heavenly peace, but also daily peace for the soul. Let us examine briefly one sentence of this Psalm composed of eight words, for within these words are found the key to relaxation—and nobody can live and maintain a healthy body or a healthy mind without learning to relax. Here are the words: "He maketh me to lie down in green pastures" . . . "I come that men might have life and that they might have it more abundantly."

We have already noted in the last chapter that, in the days of David, a good shepherd would start his sheep grazing in the morning about 3:00 A.M. They would feed until around 10:00 A.M. A good shepherd would have his grazing schedule so arranged as to arrive in the greenest and most tender grazing area at 10:00 A.M. His sheep would then lie down in the cool, green, soft grass and assimilate their food. It is in this period that the sheep put on most of their fat and develop their best wool. Denied this daily resting period, sheep will not grow fat or produce good wool. The shepherd has to make his sheep lie down . . . "He maketh me to lie down in green pastures."

Today we live and act like children on a picnic near a swimming pool. The longest period of a child's life is when he has to wait thirty minutes after eating a good picnic lunch before he can go in swimming. He cannot be restrained by the fear of drowning from cramps, and parents have to force him by their wills not to enter the water too soon after eating. This is the way the average person is living today—a life of restlessness. We approach our religion in the same restless way. We rush into the presence of God and say, "Here I am. Let us get this over with in a hurry. I am in a hurry to get back to my job or my play." We worship by the clock and pray by the minute. We do not like to lie down, even in green pastures, and so the good shepherd has to make us lie down in green pastures.

Let me suggest three types of green pastures in which we may be forced to lie down for our own good. God, knowing man's needs, has provided pastures in which his children can rest, assimilate their food, and thus grow physically and spiritually in a normal way.

Sunday was given to man in the beginning of time as a green pasture. It is the time we can assimilate spiritual energy needed to carry us over the other six days of struggle and strife of life. To use this day for any other purpose is to deny our body and soul the rest it needs to make it strong to face the tests of life. The shepherd makes his sheep lie down, even in the midst of plenty, for he knows what is good for the sheep.

God did not rest from his labors of creation on the Sabbath because he needed rest, but he did so to illustrate man's need for such a break in life's routine.

It was as natural and normal for the early Christians to worship their Christ as it was for them to retire at night for rest. It is as impossible to keep spiritually healthy and neglect worshipping God as it would be to keep healthy and neglect nightly sleep. A few quiet hours on Sunday in God's house of worship can mean the difference between a happy, healthy, spiritual person and a spiritually deformed person.

No nation that neglects God's Day of Worship remains strong in morals and in spiritual strength. One of the distressing things about our country is the way we are making Sunday more a day of business and pleasure. We have become boastful of this fact even to the point of advertising: "We never close. Open seven days a week."

Sunday is God's day. It is the day to "Lie down in His green pastures." It is God's strengthening period for man. No nation can become stronger than the way it keeps God's day, and no Christian can be stronger than the way he keeps God's Day of Worship. This day belongs to the Good Shepherd who wants to strengthen his sheep. It is the day that shall determine the nature (the success or failure) of the other six days. Spend Sunday in God's Green Valley and you will be better equipped for the responsibilities for Monday.

"Sunday is my only day to relax." How often this is used as an excuse to make Sunday the most strength-taxing day of all seven, and when the day is over, we hit our beds more bushed than on any of the other six days.

If you have ever tried this, get dressed Sunday morning and go to church somewhere. Enter the church in an expectant mood. Relax in the pew; listen quietly to the organ prelude; join in the singing of the hymns the best you can. Meditate in your own way when someone prays and try to follow the message the minister is bringing. You will go home in a happy frame of mind and really be relaxed. If you enter into this program with an honest motive, you will find that it will bring you not only a strange inner peace, but it will also make the coming week easier to live. "He maketh me to lie down in green pastures."

Sheep graze in green pastures daily. Neither man nor sheep have the capacity to eat enough in one day to last a week or a month. Some of us try one spiritual meal on Easter and try to make one prayer on Sunday last seven days. Man needs to enter green pastures and to lie down therein daily. What would happen to an engine of yesteryear if the engineer said to his fireman, "We have to cover two hundred miles on this trip. Fire up the boiler in the engine and get enough steam to carry us all the way." I would not want to be around that engine if the fireman tried to carry out those orders, for no engine is built large enough to carry that much steam. Nor does man have the spiritual capacity to carry the grace he needs beyond each day. A good fireman has enough steam in his boiler to get the train rolling at top speed, but he feeds it coal and water at certain intervals to keep it rolling.

"He maketh me to lie down in green pastures" . . . Man needs a daily relaxing period with his God. He needs to give God a chance to speak to his soul. God spoke to man in the Bible and said, "Be still and know that I am God." If you would be a well-balanced person spiritually, set aside a part of your day to be alone with God. Read a few verses of His Word, perhaps a chapter or two, and then sit quietly for a few moments and think of what you have read. Let God speak to your heart, and then bow your head and speak to Him about anything that is on your heart, and when you go from His presence, you go with His presence.

"He maketh me . . ." Here is the human element that God has to deal with in us all. David knew sheep. He knew that they did not want to rest. They wanted to continue their feeding march across the valley. He would take his staff and bring them to a halt and bed them down for a rest period. As David, with stylus in hand, paused to bring this picture back afresh to his mind, his thoughts turned from sheep to himself. How often God had to treat David as David had to treat his sheep. So many times, David found himself too busy to be still—to lie down in green pastures. Etched in the mind of David was the experience that when he became so busy with life, he forgot his God. He sinned the sin of murder and adultery. God then brought him into the green valley of despair and made him lie down. God's prophet pointed his finger in the face of the great king and said "God has seen what you have done. You shall pay for your sin. He will take the life of your child." And God did exactly that.

God makes man to lie down in many ways. Sometimes we get so busy with things of this world that we find no time to lie down in God's green pastures, so He stops us with the loss of a job, or the loss of health.

In one of my early churches I had a member who never attended, nor would he give God any of his time in service. I asked him why he did not attend church. He said, "It is nothing against you, Preacher. In fact, I like you. But you see I am too busy making a living for my family." He was a busy man. He had a grocery business; ran a post office in his town; owned and ran a saw mill; was the leading politician in the community; and had his fingers in quite a few more things. Yes, he was a very busy man. Before I turned away from him that day I asked him one question: "What would happen to your family and to your many business interests if you should die today? You are too busy to honor God in worship and service." (And that is too busy for any man to be.) The next Sunday he was in church for the first time since I had become pastor of that church. Tuesday he was in the hospital. I buried him the following week.

When I was a small child, we forgot at times that mother was watching and hearing things we said. That is, until something was done or said that should not have been. Then mother spoke in no uncertain terms and some sort of punishment followed. But those periods did as much to mold my life as any experience has done. Deep down in our hearts we knew that mother really meant it when she said before she applied the switch, "This is going to hurt me more than it will you."

The great men of God in the Bible found their greatness in the quietness of God. God had a nation and a history to make through Abraham, but God had to first lead Abraham to prove his love for God by offering his son, Isaac, to God as a sacrifice before He could draw from Abraham that nation. It was at the altar of sacrifice that Abraham proved, not to God, for God knew what he would do, but to himself, that God could trust him now without reservation. When he drew the knife to make an offering of his only son, he learned in the rays of a sun-kissed knife just how much he loved his God and what that love was costing him —his only son. Abraham went up that mountain as an obedient Jew; he came down as a father of nations.

Moses found his strength with his God in the burning bush as he talked with the angel from heaven. Paul heard Christ's voice in the flash of light from heaven. He was blinded, but given vision to see the glories of heaven as no other earthly one has seen before or since. Paul was stubborn, and this was the only way God had to get him to "lie down in green pastures" to gain the knowledge and the purpose that God had for his life

. . . "The Lord is my shepherd, I shall not want. He maketh me to lie down in green pastures."

Do you want inner peace? Lie down, then, in the green pastures of God. Relax in His presence and listen as He speaks to your heart, and you will have peace. Attend church somewhere; turn aside to be with God before you retire and meditate on His word and pray. Don't make God force you to lie down. He would rather speak through a sermon than a storm, a song rather than sickness, and through His word rather than through wretchedness.

Chapter 6

Avoid Polluted Waters

"He leadeth me beside the still waters" . . . Many explanations have been given to this oft-quoted scripture, but no scripture should be lifted from its context without first understanding or explaining the context or background. This Twenty-Third Psalm becomes a storehouse of precious treasures for the weary, the discouraged, the defeated, or for the seeker of truth—to the one who will study each line in the light of a shepherd as he relates himself to his sheep. In this series, on this greatest of all the Psalms, we are trying to take each thought as it is expressed, as keys to unlock the doors of inward peace for the soul. We believe that if one would apply each of these separate truths found in this Psalm to his own life, he would find peace.

"He leadeth me beside the still waters" . . . David had done this a thousand times for his sheep. A shepherd had to find daily pastures for his sheep, and besides the grass in those pastures, he had to locate water nearby. But sheep are not like other animals—not just any kind of water would do. Sheep will not drink from a running stream. They are afraid of running water. A shepherd must find a pool of water, a stream that has a calm channel, or he must build a small dam to catch and hold still water. Sheep must have water or they perish, but they must have water under certain conditions or they will not drink.

As David sat meditating upon his own relationship with his God, his eyes kept seeing sheep under the care of a good shepherd, and so he wrote "The Lord is my shepherd, I shall not want. He maketh me to lie down in green pastures. He leadeth me beside still waters." As I studied this phrase, three thoughts suggested themselves to me. Within them is to be found another key to unlock doors of the soul to inner peace.

The words "still waters" suggest that not all streams, nor just any kind of water, is safe for sheep to drink. There is a reason for this fear in the hearts of sheep for strange waters. God has given sheep the instinct of fear for all waters except "still waters." This God-given instinct saved many sheep from death. Sheep are poor swimmers and drown easily. They have heavy coats of wool that drag them down when wet. They cannot wade out into a fast-moving stream for their heavy bodies offer a good target for the swift current to sweep them off their small feet and to death. Some animals have little or no fear of any kind of water, but not sheep. They must have still water to drink.

I do not think it was a coincidence that the word for worship has for its root a word that means reverence based on quietness or awe. The individual yearns for spiritual quietness, for "still waters," as he drinks water for the soul. God's word says, "Be still and know that I am God." Within the hearts of all men, there is a yearning for "still waters," but like sheep, man is afraid of turbulent waters. He needs a shepherd to guide him into the still waters of God, or for someone to dam up the stream so that he might drink without fear.

Let us face this unhappy thought, for it is a fact. There are many kinds of religions in the world today. We divide all religions into ten categories. Christianity is but one of the ten great religions of the world. Within Christianity are many subdivisions. As man looks around him, and as he searches for the "still waters" for the soul, confusion and fear fill his heart. Man will not admit this fact even to himself, but actions speak louder than words. Why is it that it is so difficult to get the nonreligious to attend worship service? Why is it so difficult to get them to sit down with a minister, or a Christian worker, and discuss spiritual needs. And why is it that man shies away from all things religious? Perhaps it is because people are basically afraid of the noise man has put into religion. In the eyes of many non-Christians, religion is much like a three-ring circus.

One Saturday night, I attended an L.S.U-Kentucky football game with a businessman. He had been a Christian for three weeks. He said that this was the first football game he had really seen, for all the previous games he had attended were seen through the haze of a whiskey bottle. After the game, he said, "I watched others around me who were doing what I had done for years. How can they be so blind to the foolishness of their ways?" I reminded him how I had tried for years to point this fact out to him and how he had resisted every attempt I had made to reach him for Christ. He said simply, "I was afraid. I wanted to become a Christian, but I was afraid." "Afraid of what?" I asked, but I knew the answer before he replied. He was afraid of drinking at the wrong stream and of coming away still thirsty, or of being caught by this stream of religion and having all the joys of life drowned in it. How different it was for him when he found the "still waters" of Christ. The first words he had said to me when I drove up to his house prior to the football game were, "Dr. Carpenter, the past three weeks have been the happiest of my life." Then he added, "I have been married seventeen years and the past three weeks have been the happiest of all those seventeen years." Three weeks before, he and his wife had both drunk from the "still waters" of God together, and this made a difference in their personal lives, and changed their married life, too.

"Still waters" suggests a second thing. I discovered that in the Far East most water is not safe to drink because much of the water has become polluted. This is also becoming true of the once healthy rivers and streams of America. Water leaves the mountains pure, fresh, and cool, but when it arrives in the streams or in the pools in the valleys, some of this water is unfit for human or animal consumption. Foreign matter has entered

into it and makes this water a killer rather than a saviour. Church
history is marked by the graveyards to be found by the polluted
wells of each century. Jesus was aware of this danger, and
warned against it. Later Paul warned against this by saying that
even if the angels came preaching any other gospel, save that
which He preached, beware, for that one was a polluted mouth-
piece of God.

The church of the Living God has become many things
to many people. It has become a springboard of social ethics for
some. It has become the mark of respectability for others. God's
house has become a place for marriages and funerals for many
—nothing more. It has become a retreat from the world for those
who lack the courage to face the world. It has become a profession for some who seek position and prestige. Polluted streams,
all of them, bring to those who drink from them, spiritual death
in the end. They will carry the sheep, heavy laden, not with
wool but with sins, down its streams into a hell that has no end
or outlet. A gospel of social ethics might put new clothes on the
sinner, but it cannot wash the heart of man clean of sin. Marriage
in the House of God for two people is lovely, and the funeral
music on the church organ softens the death blow a little, but
neither opens the gates of heaven for people. Jesus said, "I am
the Way, the Truth and the Life. I am the door; there is no
other door, no other entrance into the Kingdom of God."

Sometimes I wish that it were possible to strip churches of
all denominations of their many plusses added since the first
century and start with the simple, yet pure, message of Jesus
again, for we get so involved in our promotion of organizations
denominations, etc., that we lose sight of the man in the street
who is starving for the water, the pure "still waters" of the
Gospel. We spend so much of our time and talents on erecting
great houses of worship to magnify the name of our church,
or of the minister who attracts great crowds by his ability to

handle words, that we fail to provide "still waters" for the lost sheep of God who come to such a building.

Man ought to honor God with the erection of the finest house of worship that he can. To do less would be to dishonor God, but lost man should not be sacrificed on the altar. No, not the altar of God. Christ made the last offering for man when he died on the Cross of Calvary. When we get so big, or wealthy, or so important as an individual church, we are too big to be concerned for the lost. A church can be big and still provide "still water" for the thirsty. One Sunday night I worshipped in the most beautiful and largest church in the deep South, east of the Mississippi. This new church building was just finished three weeks before. It cost between one and two million dollars. As I sat in that great house of worship, I was not lost in its size, but felt that I was brought nearer to a great God. I was not made to feel the greatness of its minister, but the greatness of God as the minister preached. It truly was a house of "still waters." It came as no surprise to me that on that particular Sunday, with no special emphasis, just a regular Sunday program, fifty-five people made decisions for God. Nor was it strange that this church with its great seating capacity, had to turn away eight hundred people from one service. Sheep, you know, go when they are thirsty, to still waters to drink.

The greatest danger we face in America today is not from Communism, nor from another depression, but it is the danger of the churches of America becoming polluted by our wealth, numbers, size, and position, that we let our pools of still waters dry up or become so polluted that those who drink from them die spiritual deaths.

There is one other thought we should consider before leaving this phrase "still waters." There is the danger of the approach to still water. The good shepherd selects the entrance to still waters for his sheep carefully, for some of his sheep are not

as strong as others, and there are lambs in the flock. If the approaches to the water are too steep, some might perish by falling.
If the water is too deep near the edge, some sheep might drop
in over their heads as they walk into the water. So steep banks
are to be avoided, and swift currents must not reach the still
waters.

What is the right approach to spiritual still waters of life?
How is man saved? These are the two most important questions
you will face in this life. They open the doors of heaven or keep
them closed to you forever. The entrance into the still waters
of God—the entrance into eternal salvation—is the most abused
and most confused thing in religion. This is indeed strange for
Jesus made no one single subject plainer than this. Listen as
Jesus explained this in the language of the shepherd. He is
speaking to men who have rejected him: "I told you, and ye
believe not; the works that I do in my Father's name, they bear
witness of me. But ye believe not, because ye are not my sheep,
as I said unto you. My sheep hear my voice and I know them,
and they follow me; and I give unto them eternal life; and they
shall never perish, neither shall any man pluck them out of my
hand. My Father, which gave them me is greater than all, and
no man is able to pluck them out of my Father's hand. I and
my Father are one." (John 10:25-29). Jesus says, "For God so
loved the world that He gave His only begotten Son that whosoever believeth in Him should not perish but hath everlasting
life." (John 3:16).

To be saved, one must have the capacity to know, believe,
and understand. This would rule out entrance into the Kingdom
of God of those who refuse to accept the facts about Jesus. The
Bible teaches that before a child reaches the age of accounta-
bility, he is not held responsible, but that when the child reaches
the age to know right from wrong, he must decide for himself.
He must accept the fact that Christ was God's son, sent to earth,
and lived and died on the cross for man's sin; He arose on the

third day, and is now alive with the Heavenly Father. Man must then accept this act of God and Christ into his life. This is done by each of us making our own profession of faith, for each must believe for himself, and each must act for himself. Not to believe in Christ and not to accept the offering of Himself for our sin debt is to be lost, condemned. But to accept it is to drink of the "still waters" of God. Profession of faith in God is made before man. It is not a private profession between you and God. Christ said you must profess me before man. Then man is ready for baptism and church membership. The good shepherd knows that his sheep need water, and that they must have a safe place to enter the water. For in seeking life-giving water, they might lose their lives in sight of the water itself. Jesus knew this truth and so he provided the easiest plan possible for all men of all ages. No man need say to God someday, "I wanted to drink of the still waters for which my soul longed. I knew what I wanted, but I could not reach this water."

"He leadeth me beside the still waters" . . . Yes, the Good Shepherd does even today, but the sheep must drink the water if their thirst is to be satisfied. So will you.

CHAPTER 7

Sheep Must Drink to Live

In the previous chapter, we noticed that sheep were afraid of running waters. In this, the Shepherd's Psalm, the Twenty-Third, we noted why God gave sheep their inherited fear of running water. Their heavy wool would drag the sheep to their death if caught in swift, running water. Their small feet provide little or no support for swimming. Sheep are afraid of running water and a good shepherd will always find "still waters" for them from which his sheep can drink.

"The Lord is my shepherd, I shall not want. He maketh me to lie down in green pastures. He leadeth me beside the still waters." Of course, the author of the Psalm was not thinking about sheep, but of man and his relationship to God. David was drawing from his boyhood experiences as a shepherd and passing these events on to other generations—consoling messages for the weary soul. Let us examine another truth from this shepherd Psalm and from the phrase "still waters" that can unlock the door of the soul so that "the peace that passeth all understanding" might come in.

All sheep must drink water, and they will drink some kind of water if they are not led to the safety of still waters. Thirst is the strongest of all compelling drives of man or animal. Man is created with an eternal thirst for water. Thirst will drive both man and beast to drink even poisoned waters, although man might know that which he might be drinking endangers his life. Men who are shipwrecked at sea often drink salt water from the sea, driven to it by their compelling thirst, even though they know that to drink is to die. I have seen men in Africa drink from polluted wells, knowing that they were chancing illness and even death. They still drank.

There is no man without some form of religion. I picked up a *National Geographic* magazine one day and thumbed through it without reading it. One section was given over to an ancient tribe of people from one of the Pacific Ocean areas. Some of these pictures showed them building a temple. Their methods of building were crude ones and they were using primitive materials. This question pressed itself upon my mind: "Where did they get their idea of God or of gods?" Oh, I know that it came from their fathers who, in turn, got it from their fathers, and so on back. But when you reach back into the darkness of their past, you would find a belief in some form of religion—some form of God.

Even those who claim to be nonreligious have some kind of religion. In the secret places of man's heart, he has an altar of some sort before which he bows. All men are born with a spiritual thirst. They will drink at some stream in their attempt to satisfy this thirst. It must break the heart of God, as He looks down at man on this earth running to and fro, searching for spiritual water, overlooking the pure, and drinking that which has no life-giving substance. Jesus must have had somewhat the same feeling as he stood overlooking the city of Jerusalem, the day he cried over the city. He thought of God's effort to save his chosen people; He thought of the great prophets He had raised up for them, and now here was the very Son of God Himself, being rejected by them. No wonder He wept that day!

There are many streams from which men drink and die. Paul drank deeply and frequently at the rivers of tradition, but this water that he drank only clouded his spiritual vision so that when he came face to face with pure water, he could not, and did not know that it was pure. It took miracles of the Damascus Road to open the spiritual eyes of Paul to the real fountain of life. The Bible, itself, warns against the danger of traditions.

The Word of God—the Bible—is the only tradition man needs to know, and it will reveal to him where still waters of the soul are located.

The Greeks drank from the rivers of mythology. They gave the world art and literature, but they died in their own streams. The Romans drank from the streams of their gods of harvest, of the sea, half-man and half-god, and worshipped Caesar, and rejected the Lord of Lords and King of Kings. We look back at these pagan worshippers and shake our heads, but are we any better than they? We have our rivers of spiritual waters, too. Some men drink at the fountains of money, of social, business, or political gods. What is a god? It is the object, thing, or person to whom you give the inner devotions, to whom you yield yourself in service, loyalties, and affections. It is the thing, person, or object which is the focal point of your life.

Sheep cannot drink from a poison stream without paying the price. Wrong streams inflict their own penalty. Millions in America make some claim of religion, and yet, what is their religion producing in their lives? Sweet, still, pure water produces in sheep satisfaction, peace, contentment. Sheep leave still waters refreshed and ready to return to the pasture for feeding or to a night's rest. They were thirsty and drank. Now they are satisfied. What does your religion produce in your life? Peace? Contentment? Happiness?

As I think about this, two men come to my mind. I talked with both of them during the past weeks. One said to me in substance, "Let's not kid ourselves. I am not getting anything out of my religion. I go to church; give to my church, but I have no sense of peace or security. My church membership means nothing to me." He had gone into the stream of church membership and had drunk deeply, but it did not satisfy the spiritual longings of his soul. He would be classified by his minister and others as a good church member, and respected by them as such. But the test of the water he had drunk was within his own heart.

Jesus said, "My peace I give unto you. Not as the world giveth, give I unto you." Sheep come up from drinking the still waters satisfied, contented, and with their thirst quenched. This man was still thirsty, and he was lacking the peace of God within.

The second man said this, "I never knew that it would be like this. I have never been so happy and contented in my life. I have never gotten such happiness from life. I know that I am saved. I cannot explain it, but I know I am a different man now." Both men were about the same age, about equal in their business success, and about the same socially. Put them together and they could have been brothers as far as their position in this world could be measured. The difference? What each had accepted into his life to satisfy his spiritual thirst. Men will drink something to quench their spiritual thirst.

Let me suggest three things about the still waters offered by God through Christ. Study them carefully for they will lead you to the only safe water for man to drink—the only kind of water that satisfies the soul of man and quenches the thirst that God plants in the soul of every human being.

It is safe to drink and will satisfy every demand of the world because the "still waters" of Christ come from the very heart of God. "God so loved the world that He gave His only begotten Son, that whosoever believeth, should not perish, but have everlasting life." (John 3:16). Jesus said that anyone who came and drank of Him . . . would never thirst, and he came to bring the "Living Water." Christ did not create "living water," he only brought it from the throne of God the Father. Jesus was only the riverbed that brings the water to man. The fountain of living waters, still waters, finds its source in the great love of God. "For God so loved the world, that he gave" . . . It is safe for men to drink because it comes from God. And God can be trusted, for He created man, the world, and all that dwells therein.

Not only is salvation from the heart of God—still waters for the soul—but this water, this salvation, has been purified by and with the blood of the Lamb of God. The Bible says there can be no forgiveness, no purging from sin, no freedom from our sins without the shedding of blood. The supreme function of the high priest as set forth in the Bible was to make such an offering for the sins of his people. God keeps His own laws because God makes no laws which are not right or not in keeping with His nature. God passed a law against sin—"The soul that sinneth shall surely die." God's great love for mankind caused him to go a step further. He provided forgiveness from sin, based on someone paying the penalty for sin.

Offerings were made for sins of man. These were blood offerings made on the altars of the temple—not blood offerings by the sinner, but offerings of animals without physical blemish. But all these offerings had no power to fulfill the demands of God against the sins of man. They were but types of the one offering to be made by Christ, the Son of God. When the forerunner of Christ, John the Baptist, was preaching on the banks of the Jordan, he looked up one day and saw Jesus approaching. John said a strange thing; a thing that no one understood at the time, and I doubt if John, who was speaking under the inspiration of the Holy Spirit, understood it in all its fullness. He said, "Behold the Lamb of God which taketh away the sin of the world." Not "sins," but *The Sin*. Offerings made before were offered for the sins of the people or for the sins of an individual. Jesus came to be the sin offering for the human race . . . not just *an* offering for sins, as such. He came to wipe out the entire sin debt, to remove its nature from the human race. He bought the entire sin debt of the human race. He had to do this. He had to possess it if he were to declare man free from sin. Satan held man in bondage to himself by this sin debt. Jesus had no more right to say to a sinner, "Your debt is forgiven," than you would have the right to say to me, "Your debt that you owe on your house is forgiven by me, and you no longer owe the bank."

But if you should go to the bank and buy my note, then you could say to me "I paid for your note, and I own it. I now will destroy it and you owe me nothing." The death of Christ on the cross was that kind of transaction. Jesus bought our sin debt so that he could say to any one seeking salvation, "I now can forgive your sin debt charged against you." "Behold the Lamb of God which taketh away the sin of the world." It was the blood of Christ that made pure the waters of life. It is this "still water" that satisfies the soul of man.

Man is now lost, not because he is a sinner nor because he is part of the sin-infected human race. He is lost because he has not accepted the offered pardon purchased by the Son of God on Calvary. This is why the New Testament says over and over again, "Believe in the Lord Jesus Christ and thou shalt be saved." This is why Jesus said, "If you confess me before men (acknowledge that you have accepted the sin offering I made for you) I will confess you before my Heavenly Father, but if you are ashamed to confess me before men, I will also be ashamed to confess you before my Heavenly Father."

You can drink safely from this stream of pure water, and it is the only safe place to drink because this stream comes from the heart of God himself, and is perfect for the cleansing of every sin of the human heart by and through the sin offering of the blood of the precious Son of God, Jesus Christ. "The Lord is my shepherd. I shall not want. He maketh me to lie down in green pastures. He leadeth me beside the still waters." Yes, God does lead us by the still waters. He is doing this right now to any who might be reading this book, but that is all that God can do for you. You must drink of the water provided for you if you are to realize the inner peace of the soul; if you are to have eternal peace with God. "My peace I give unto you." You must accept that which is offered. You must drink to have within you the "still waters" of the soul—to have eternal life.

Now for one brief, but important, thought. I said that there were three reasons for confidence with which we can drink of the spiritual water offered by Christ. This streams from the heart of God, purified by the precious blood of His Son and God offers no other plan for man's salvation. It has been almost two thousand years since the birth of Christ. God has made no other revelation of himself, or of any new plan since the return of Christ to heaven. Men have tried to make many changes in this plan of salvation, but heaven has been silent on the matter. Now a contract still stands until it is changed by mutual agreement. The words "New Testament" means "new contract." Not only was it a new one to replace the old one, but it is the last one to be offered to man. God is just and righteous, and he must accept all those of us who appear before Him with this contract in our hands. The final test will be found within your own soul when you come and drink for yourself. "The Lord is my shepherd. I shall not want. He maketh me to lie down in green pastures. He leadeth me beside the still waters." Drinking at the still waters is a key to inner peace for which all men long. Do you have this peace today?

CHAPTER 8

Spiritual Coffee Breaks

An obliging husband found himself standing on top of a box which, in turn, was on top of a kitchen chair, hanging pictures for his wife. As he tried to drive a nail into the wall, he swayed back and forth in a precarious way. His faithful wife, watching his attempts to drive the nail into the wall with gentle taps, said to him, "Why don't you give the nail one healthy blow and be done with the job?" He replied, "How can anyone strike a healthy blow standing on such a wobbly foundation?"

This is the picture of many of us today. We are trying to live at our best, standing on a wobbly foundation. We are not sure of our position with man nor with God. Man needs to re-examine the foundation upon which he is building his life, if he finds his own reflection in this story. There can be no success in any field without a feeling of security and assurance that life is not being wasted. Such assurance is not as elusive as one might think.

It is the purpose of this series on the Twenty-Third Psalm to help you find the keys that will open for you the doors to inner peace. In the phrase "He restoreth my soul" there is another one of these keys. Let us walk among the sheep, and see through the eyes of David what he can teach us about peace of soul.

Those who know sheep say that the sheep of the Holy Lands are superior and excel other sheep in their herding instincts. David knew his sheep, and he included in this Shepherd Psalm various characteristics of his sheep. Each has a twofold meaning; one for us and one for the sheep. For example, in the phrase

"He restoreth my soul" we have expressed the need of sheep for daily assurance from their shepherd. They have slept; now they move out to the new pasture. Each sheep will take a particular spot in line and stay in that position all day. But during the day, they do an odd thing. Each sheep, at some time during the day, will leave his position with the sheep and go to the shepherd. He will nuzzle the shepherd with his nose or head and get his attention, and, in turn, the shepherd will stroke the head of the sheep for a few minutes. The sheep will then return to his former position with the other sheep, contented for the day. This is an assurance period for the sheep that seems to satisfy him for the day. "The Lord is my shepherd, I shall not want. He maketh me to lie down in green pastures. He leadeth me beside the still waters. He restoreth my soul." He refreshes my soul with his assurance. He lets me know that he is near and all is well. This is a period of reassurance for the sheep. Man, too, needs this daily assurance as he tries to face a world filled with uncertainties, unknown dangers, and forces that have the capability to destroy him. This leads us to the thought for this chapter. If man is to be reassured by God, man, himself, must seek out these periods for assurance. A shepherd cannot force this action from his sheep. He must wait until they come to him seeking his personal touch. They make the overture.

All kinds of sheep do not do this. The kind of sheep that do are marked by three things. You can make the application to your own life as we study these characteristics of the sheep who are contented and who live happily.

The contented sheep, the sheep with daily assurance, are the ones that remain in the shepherd's flock. Straying sheep do not do this—only herding sheep. Each morning they take up the position they will hold all day. They leave this place only to go to the shepherd for assurance, and after receiving this assurance, they return to their grazing position. They maintain this position when they enter into still waters for drink, or when the wolf or the bear attacks. They are sheep who have learned that safety and contentment is determined by position with their shepherd. They have learned that each flock of sheep has a shepherd whose job is to care for them.

Man cannot find happiness for himself outside the fold of God. Millions of books have been printed to point man to the ways of finding peace within himself, and peace with other men. There can be no lasting or abiding peace for any man until he has learned the will of God for himself. God does have for all men a pattern for their lives—a pattern that would give them the most from life if they would live within it.

'Tis the sheep of the flock—not the stray sheep—who are fat and carry wool. It is the sheep of the flock that are healthy and that raise the finest lambs. 'Tis the sheep of the flock that are fed the finest grass, and drink the sweetest water, for they are the "cared for" sheep. They have a shepherd to find the best grass and the sweetest water for them.

For some strange reason, most men fear the will of God for their lives. They seem to be afraid to trust themselves into His Hands. This is very strange, for history gives us no grounds for this fear. No one who has ever totally committed himself to the will of God has ever regretted doing so.

Some time ago, I sat talking with a man in a southern city. He had made an unsuccessful attempt to take his own life. He was a young man, with most of his life ahead of him. He was a man with ability and promise, but he had lost his grip on life and tried to take the easy way out. It did not take long for the real cause of this act to come to the surface. He was not willing to let himself go and let God take over the reins of his life. Later I talked with his wife and found that she, too, had a similar problem. Deep down in their hearts they were afraid to live within the will of God; to take their own hands off their lives, and let God be their shepherd in every sense of the word.

Oftentimes, man makes the mistake of trying to substitute

something else for God's will. He will join some church and
try to substitute this for God's will for himself. Many of these
people become just another name on some church roll. Perhaps,
there is no more evangelistic denomination in the world today
than Southern Baptist. They are baptizing new converts at the
rate of more than a million every three years. This is wonderful!
Yes, it is, but when one takes a second look at their church rolls
and realize there are more than 1,750,000 names of people they
cannot locate because of lack of an address, we are staggered
by what this suggests—substituting church membership for God's
will. For if they were living within the will of God, they would
stay within the flock of God—at least to the point of having an
active address. Where are these 1,750,000 people? They have
moved into new cities, bought new homes, gone into new busi-
nesses, joined new clubs, but have so little interest in their church
memberships that they do not deem it important enough to
inform their church back home of their present address. This
is not an indictment against Southern Baptists. A similar study
of other religions in America will reveal the same story.

Oh yes, man has found one of a thousand things to substitute for God's will in his life. It might be a fat bank account;
success in business; the whirl of society; or it might be a bottle
of sleeping pills at night to ease a restless conscience. It matters
not what it might be. Man cannot find peace for his soul outside
the will of God, and this will of God needs daily assurance from
God. To have this assurance, the sheep seeks out his shepherd
each day at least once. "He restoreth my soul." He refreshes me
with assurance that he is still my shepherd. The mark of a contented sheep is that he lives within the flock—within the will
of the shepherd.

There is a second characteristic of a contented sheep. The
sheep has no fear of his shepherd. This is why he comes to the
shepherd. Prayer is the greatest gift from God to man aside from
salvation itself. Prayer is the most powerful force God has placed

in man's hand—more powerful than the atom bomb. It is one of the easiest things for us to do. It takes no college training to pray. It takes no great physical effort. A lame man or a small child can pray. It is one of the most satisfying things a Christian can do, and yet, prayer is the most neglected thing in religion. Though it offers the highest dividends, the average Christian gets the poorest results from his prayer life than he does from any one thing in his religion. The average church member spends less than five minutes praying each day. Why doesn't man pray more often and longer? Here is the answer. Man is afraid to approach his God even in prayer. Why is he afraid? He is ashamed of his dirty hands, mind, and soul. He knows that he cannot fool God.

When was the last time you really prayed to God? How much time do you spend each day in prayer? Search your heart and be honest with yourself, and you will be shocked by what you find within your own life.

Sheep come to their shepherd to be assured that they are still his sheep; that he is still near them, and that he still stands watch over them. They want to know that he still loves them, and what is just as important, they want him to know that they are his sheep, and they are saying to him in their own way, "We love you, too."

You can search the Bible through and you will not find one word of condemnation for sheep by a shepherd. You see, a shepherd loves his sheep, even to the point of giving his own life to protect his sheep. Do you recall the story of the ninety-nine sheep, safe in the fold, and the one lost sheep out in the blackness of the night as told by Jesus? What happened when the shepherd found the lost sheep? Did the shepherd scold him for causing the hardships he had suffered in finding him? Did he whip the lost sheep to teach him a lesson? Did he say, "I should have left you in the darkness to die, for you were a bad sheep and did not appreciate my care?" He did not say any of these things.

He put the sheep, cold and frightened, on his own shoulders and returned to the sheepfold rejoicing over finding the lost one alive. You see, he loved that sheep, good or bad, lost or safe within the fold. He loved him.

Again, we cannot understand why man is afraid of God—but he is; the evidence of this fear is visible to all by man's refusal to come to God for forgiveness. Search the Bible from cover to cover. Not one time will you find Christ rebuking anyone who comes seeking, asking for forgiveness. Sheep, who are happy and content, who stay within the fold, are not afraid of their shepherd.

No man can be really happy and contented in this life and live in fear of God. God does not want man to fear him but to love him. Fear and love cannot live in the same house. One will destroy the other. Jesus once said to his disciples, "Fear not." This means, in the original language, "Stop being afraid of me. Be not afraid. It is I." If you are afraid to approach God, go to him in prayer and tell him about your fears. Show him your dirty hands. Open your unclean heart to him and throw yourself upon his mercy. You will find yourself on the shoulders of the Good Shepherd and hear him say, "Rejoice, that which was lost is found again." And you will find a new and wonderful peace flooding your soul. You will have peace of soul, for your fear of God will be gone.

I said in the beginning of this chapter, contented and happy are the sheep living within the flock, within the will of the shepherd. They have no fear of the shepherd. Therefore, remember that such sheep go to the shepherd—the shepherd does not go to the sheep. They must make the overture and the shepherd will respond—he never fails to respond. Man only has to take one step toward God, and God does the rest. Have you ever approached one of those doors to a building that is controlled by a "magic eye" and opens automatically when you cross an invisible light ray? You feel like reaching out to push open the door, only to find it flying open before your hands reach it. This is the spiritual experience of every person reaching out for the hand of God. He finds the door wide open to the eternal grace of God, and to peace—eternal and abiding peace.

A student at Wellesley College said of Alice Freeman Palmer, the second president of Wellesley, "When I was called into her office, either for commendation, a social visit, or for a reprimand, I left her office and her presence feeling as if I had been dipped in sunshine." A few moments spent each day with the Master will give you peace. "He restoreth my soul."

CHAPTER 9

The Key of Peace—
Wherein You Walk

Galileo, the great Italian scientist, once said, "I have noticed that the sun which holds the whirling stars, planets and worlds in place in the universe, also has time to ripen a bunch of grapes on the vines of Italy."

We noticed in our last chapter that sheep of the Holy Land have a peculiar habit. Each morning they take a certain place in line with the other sheep and leave this place only once. That is when they take turns to go to their shepherd to rub their noses against his body and to receive, in turn, a pat and a rub from his hands. They then return to their places with the other sheep to remain contented the rest of the day. This habit of the sheep caused David to pen these lines in the Twenty-Third Psalm, "He restoreth my soul. He leadeth me in the paths of righteousness for his name's sake."

It mattered not how large a herd of sheep a shepherd had under his care. He always had time to give each individual sheep the attention he needed. Galileo observed with great amazement that even though the sun had great tasks to perform in God's universe, it also had time to ripen a bunch of grapes in Italy. Without this personal attention of the sun, there would be no ripe grapes in Italy, or anywhere else. Yet, some men try to tell us that God is too great and too busy to be concerned with the personal problems of his children. Would God do less for one of his own children than a shepherd would do for one of his sheep? Would God do less for one of his precious sons or daughters than the sun, a creation of his hands, would do for a bunch of unripened grapes in Italy?

Sheep seem to say to their shepherd by his act of reassurance, "Thank you, shepherd, for the care of the night, and thank you for the promise of protection for this day. We look to you for cool, quiet, refreshing water when we are thirsty, and for green pastures in the heat of the day." But it is more than an act of their devotion and appreciation; it is an expression of their complete confidence in Him as their shepherd. "He leadeth me in the paths of righteousness for His name's sake." This suggests three things to us. No sheep can be happy walking out of the paths selected by the shepherd for his sheep. No shepherd would dare lead his sheep over a dangerous path when there is a safe path to take. He would not lead his sheep into swift-moving waters to drink. No shepherd would lead his sheep into areas where the wolf or bear or the lion lurked. No shepherd would expose his sheep at night to the hidden dangers, but would build a sheepfold to give them the maximum protection. Would God do less for his own?

Sheep follow the paths of their shepherd—follow them gladly and without fear. "For His name's sake." The name of the shepherd is held in high esteem in the Far East. To flee from the approaching lion, or to leave the sheep to the cruel jaws of the wolf, would be the height of shame for a shepherd. The very name "shepherd" calls for him to die defending his sheep rather than fleeing to save his own life without his sheep. Sheep know this by instinct, and are happy following the path of their shepherd.

When the first breath of cold air touches the geese and ducks feeding in the far north, something stirs within their breasts; a restlessness possesses them, and sends them into the air to fly in the direction—south. When the northern lakes and rivers begin to thaw, these same geese and ducks, many thousands of miles to the south, feel a tug in their hearts again, and they return north once more. They have learned by some unexplained reason that happiness for them is to be found following this unseen leadership. Those who refuse to do so soon die of starvation when their source of food is covered over with ice and snow. Safety for them rests within the will of their creator. What a pity that man has not learned this simple lesson. God never leads one astray or into unhappiness. "He leadeth me in the paths of righteousness," and this word "righteousness" means not spiritual goodness here, but means in the paths which are right, safe, and good for me to travel.

God's men in every generation have pleaded with individuals in all walks of life to seek, and then live within the will of God for themselves. They have tried to get nations to do the same, and yet, men continue to reject the fact that God's leadership is better than their own. I have talked with many unhappy people, and I have found that beneath most of the unhappiness is the failure to live or to know the will of God for themselves. Every unhappiness among human beings can be traced to the failure to live within the will of God who has their welfare at heart.

To many people, God is no more than a hidden traffic policeman eagerly waiting to catch the first speeder who comes along, and is disappointed if one does not show up before he goes off duty. You will find no such picture of God in the New Testament. God does not want to arrest, try, nor punish anyone; no, he wants to direct them onto the right road of life—the road that leads to a place of importance and value—a road of peace, safety, and happiness.

God has never made a mistake, nor should any man be afraid that he will be God's first mistake. Do not flatter yourself with such a thought. God knows that there can be no lasting happiness for man outside of His perfect will for man.

Whenever I baptized a person of advanced years, it was not uncommon to hear him say, "I should have done this years ago. If I had done so, I would have saved myself many years of unhappiness and misery. I cannot understand why I waited so long to make this important decision." They are saying what sheep know—there is no happiness outside the will of the shepherd.

Sheep have learned a second thing about walking in the paths of righteousness—the paths selected by the shepherd for them. Happiness, peace, and contentment on the trails, in the fields, or in the valleys does not come from the trails they are traveling but comes from the one with whom they are traveling. Their happiness comes from their closeness with the shepherd. They know he is near, with eyes trained to detect the slightest movement that would suggest danger to them. His ears are alert to hear the sudden disturbed quietness of the flock which means that danger is near. They know that before anything can get to them, it must get by him.

Watch sheep feeding under the care of a shepherd. They give all their attention to their feeding. They enter into a quiet pool to drink without fear of what might be lurking on the banks of the stream. They do this for they know their shepherd is near, and he is watching over them.

The average professed Christian lives and acts as if God were on a permanent vacation. No wonder we are living in an age of nervous breakdowns, of human misery and shattered faiths. We have lost the assurance of the presence of the shepherd. Sheep are contented and happy as long as they have their shepherd near. His very closeness is their assurance. "He leadeth me in the paths of righteousness." He does not order his sheep into some strange new path. No, not a good shepherd. He leads them into it. He goes on ahead to clear the way, and stands by as they pass through. You recall that Jesus said, "Lo, I am with you even unto the end of the ages—ages without end."

The late Rear Admiral Byrd of Virginia, told of getting lost from his hut at the South Pole. He knew that he could not find his way back in the vastness and whiteness of the world he was in and that he could wander around in circles until he dropped from exhaustion and exposure. He knew he must have some point that would give him direction, and so he stuck a pole in the snow and put his colored scarf on top of the pole and struck out in a direction, traveling as far as he thought he needed to travel to reach his snow covered hut. He never got out of sight of the pole, and would return to it if he did not find his hut in that direction. He returned to his pole four times before he located his hut. He said, "I would have died and would have been helpless to save myself had it not been for the pole. It became the center of my life until I found my hut." Then he added, "Every life needs a center—something to guide it—something we can be certain about."

Sheep are happy because they have their shepherd to guide them in the right paths. They have him as the center of their lives. They can be sure of him for he is the center of their lives.

One of the many books that came out about World War II was one entitled *And God Was There*. It was written by a combat chaplain who had gathered personal experiences from many of his men as they lived through the hell of war. This book painted the desperate plight of men fighting for their lives, caught many times in situations which seemed hopeless. But time after time, with all hope gone, these men would say, "But God is here; God is here." Many did not live to tell what they meant by those words, but those of us who were with such men knew. It mattered not how brutal, how hellish, how desperate the situation was, there was always a divine oasis near us—those of us who knew the Lord through His Son Christ Jesus, and from this oasis, we drank from the fountain of peace. "He leadeth me in the paths of righteousness." Through the right paths for us to travel—being led by the Good Shepherd—we find peace in His presence.

Thought number one—there can be no peace, nor security for sheep, if they walk not in the paths chosen for them by the

Good Shepherd. Thought number two—walking with the Good Shepherd brings its own peace. His very presence is our peace, is our security and our joy.

Now this last thought. Sheep get their peace walking in the paths chosen by their shepherd because it is his path—they are within his path—and this gives them the assurance of well-being. It is like being in a warm, comfortable home during a wintry storm. Being in a warm, snug house under such circumstances brings its own joy.

This happiness or contentment of the sheep comes not from walking well or successfully in God's chosen path, but from being on it. They might stumble over the ruts at times and even become bruised by the roughness of the path, but these are taken in stride, for being on the right path is reward enough.

The next time you attend a football game, look at the bench of players who are not in the game. Some of the men might not get into a single game all year, and might not even earn a letter for all their effort and sacrifice. You ask yourself why they go through all the hard work, take all the bruises they have to take, and know that they might never see their names on the sports page of their paper? There is not one man on that bench who would swap places with any man in the stadium! Oh, yes, they would give anything to be the star of each game and have their names headlined on the sports pages of the country, but they know this cannot be, and they feel well-paid for their efforts by just being a member of their school team.

Being in the flock brings its own reward. Living within the path God has set for your life brings its own joy. Our joy comes from being with the right crowd—God's crowd—traveling on God's road with God as our leader. This will fill to the brim the cup of the soul, and will satisfy. "He leadeth me in the paths of righteousness for His name's sake." This was the victory shout of the Psalmist.

I remember well one fall day when our football coach picked

the varsity football team for the season. We had worked very hard for several weeks getting in shape, learning plays and formations. When we had finished the practice for the day, he called us around him and took out a list and began to read. When he called out my name, and I knew that I was now on the team, a warm feeling of peace came into my heart. Oh, I knew there would be days of hard work ahead, but I did not mind that, for I was on the team—I had made it—and this was reward in itself.

This is the kind of peace David was talking about—the peace that comes when we know that we are being led by the Good Shepherd, and know it is true with our own lives that "He leadeth me in the paths of righteousness for His name's sake."

On the eve of a great battle, Napoleon would summon his generals into his presence. One by one they would pass from an anteroom into the chamber where Napoleon waited for them; and each man, as he came, would find Napoleon standing to greet him, with Napoleon's hand outstretched towards him, and Napoleon's eyes looking into his own. And each man would go to his battlestation with the strength of ten within him, and the feeling that there was no exploit that lay beyond his powers that day.

The people that do know their God and wait upon Him day after day and see His face and feel His hand clasp their own—they shall go from His presence into the world where they are called to do battle for His Name, "strong in the Lord of hosts and in His mighty power." They shall say in most hearts, "I can do all things through Him that strengthens me."

CHAPTER 10

Don't Let the Shadows of Life Upset You

David was familiar with a certain valley called the "Valley of Death" when he wrote the Twenty-Third Psalm. There is such a place in Palestine. It is south of the Jericho Road and leads from the Dead Sea to Jerusalem. This valley is four and a half miles long and is fifteen hundred feet in depth. The path leading through this valley is so narrow that it must be used as a one-way road for there can be no passing, and the fifteen hundred foot drop means death to man or animal. Sheep pass through it during the season to get to new pastures. They are taken up through it in the morning by their shepherd and down in the afternoon. This schedule is observed by all. At one place on this path, there is a gap of eighteen inches where the sheep have to jump across. Only man and animal can travel this path. Wild dogs and other animals lurk near this roadway to catch the strays or to snatch off an animal from the trail when the shepherd gets careless. Shepherds fight off these destructive animals with their staffs, knocking them off the road into the valley below. David had this path in mind when he wrote, "Yea, though I walk through the valley of the shadow of death, I will fear no evil. Thy rod and thy staff they comfort me." Jesus said, "I am the good shepherd. The good shepherd giveth his life for his sheep."

Man does not walk in the valley of death in this world just on certain occasions, such as during a war or when he has to perform some dangerous task. No, man does not walk in such

87

valleys only then. He lives in and among such valleys every day of his life. He is not equipped to defend himself from all the dangers he must face because he is not even aware of them. Man needs a shepherd to stand guard over him—a shepherd who knows where such dangers are and how to deal with each: "The Lord is my shepherd." He travels the highways of life with me, watching for the forces that would drag me off the paths of life into destruction. This is, indeed, a wonderful thought. Yes, it is more than a thought. It is a fact, a truth, a reality—a fact that can lighten the heart of every man.

Let us notice some of the valleys of death that we must travel in this life. There are valleys with hidden killers on every side; killers that cannot be seen until they have taken their toll of human lives. These are emotional valleys of death. I recently read an article in one of our national magazines called, "Is There Hope for the Living Dead?" It dealt with the many hundreds of thousands of people who are caught without notice by the killer of the emotional stability of man. It strikes among all people of all ages regardless of their race, color, or creed, and regardless of their backgrounds. It can snatch from society the brilliant mind or the average person. One out of every four persons is affected to some degree by this valley of emotional death.

Man was created by God as an emotional creature. Our emotions play an important part in our lives. We cannot totally suppress our emotions without damage to the personality. We express our emotions in many ways, the most familiar being through tears or laughter. We might think of hate or of love with our minds, but we feel hate and love through our emotions and give them a free ride from the inside to the outside of our lives through the railroad of our emotions. If Satan can sabotage these emotional railroads in our lives, if we do it ourselves, or if certain forces in life do this, there will be a wreck of our emotional trains. Damage can be as slight as a derailment of a single car or as great as the destruction of the train itself.

There are at least three great periods of emotional danger for us in life. These periods can be likened to the shepherd taking his sheep from one pasture to another through the valley of the shadow of death in Palestine. We need the Good Shepherd to take us through these valleys if we want to be assured of safe travel. To try to tread these roads without God is a dangerous thing. You might get through, but many do not without some damage being done. "Yea, though I walk through the valley of the shadow of death, I will fear no evil. Thy rod and thy staff they comfort me."

There are great periods of stress and strain during times of radical changes in life—periods when great choices are thrust upon us. Youth encounters one of these periods when they approach the door of manhood or womanhood. They must choose a career, a mate, and the place they hope to fill in this world. They pass out from under the shelter of parents into a world they must face alone. They need a shepherd during this period to guide them. Youth will find some kind of a shepherd. We have seen what happened to the youth of a nation when they chose a political madman like Hitler for their leader. Our jails reveal the folly of following a wrong shepherd. This is the period of time when many parents lose their children to the world. A period when many hasty marriages are made, marriages to escape from an unhappy home. This is a period of "no shepherd" and a period in which seeds are planted that shall bring forth a harvest of unhappiness in the years ahead. A good shepherd is needed by all youth as they approach this period.

I have had conferences with many hundreds of young people who are passing through this stress period. It breaks one's heart to look into their minds and see the struggle some are having to keep their feet going in the right direction. So many lack the proper spiritual guidance they ought to have had and should have received from their parents. Some parents teach their children how to smoke the right brand of cigarettes, how to buy the right kind of clothes and how to wear them properly, and how to choose the right kind of people to associate with, but fail to point out to their children, by example or by teaching, the Good Shepherd. Their children must walk through the valleys of death without a shepherd because of this parental failure.

It always thrills this writer's heart when he has united in marriage two fine young people. They have chosen each other under the watchful eyes of the Good Shepherd, and now they start out on their life together, still under His leadership. Such a marriage will never end up in a divorce court for their shepherd will not lead them that way.

We pass through another emotional valley of death as we enter into old age. This is another period of stress and strain for man. What I mean by "old age" is not old age itself, but the approach to it. So many people fear the approaching years, with each year increasing this dread. For those who have walked through life under the loving care of the Good Shepherd, they find nothing in the fleeing years to fill them with fear, for they know that He has always supplied them with the things they needed to make life useful and happy, and they know that He will continue to provide for them throughout *every* year of their lives.

One day I sat talking with a wonderful old man. He had been extremely successful in the business world and is a wonderful Christian. As I watched him drive away in his car, I thought to myself, "He has only a few years left to live. Even if God gives him a few extra years, what does he have to live for, and how can he be so happy when he knows that very soon he must leave all that he has accumulated?" Of course, I knew the answer. He has lived, and was living, under the watchful eyes of the Good Shepherd, and being with Him daily through the years had prepared him for the future—even for death, itself.

A third emotional "valley of death" is the time when tragedies of life come to us. These will come to all of us. It comes to some in the loss of good health, in the death of a loved one, in the loss of a job, the failure of a friend to be true, or in a thousand other forms.

I have a friend in another state who has lived a bitter life for years, and as far as I know, if he is still alive, his life is still bitter. This bitterness has robbed him of the joys of life with his family and friends and his usefulness to his church and his community. His firstborn son became ill one day and, through his medical ignorance, he gave the child the wrong kind of medicine. The boy died. He blamed God for this loss. He shut the doors of his heart so tightly that no one could get in. He was without a shepherd, and walked through this valley of death alone. You say, "But this is an extreme example." Yes, it is, but there are many more I could mention. Look around you. There are many people similar to this man. Many have drifted out of their church. Many have become lost to the service of their Master, just because some other church member failed them in a crisis. Some have fallen victims to broken faith in others. Others have had their lives shattered because a husband or wife broke faith with their marriage and became emotional driftwood on the sea of life, to be washed upon some strange shore of uselessness.

Every minister knows that he cannot please all his people. He knows, too, that often, in trying to do that which is right, his actions are misunderstood and, at times, even thought to be wrong. He is human and cannot be exempt from error. This is why he tries to point men toward the Good Shepherd rather than toward himself as their ideal and their guide. Ministers might (and do, at times) fail their people, but the Good Shepherd never fails. His staff is long enough to reach out to the last sheep in His flock and draw it back from the brink of complete despair, and his rod is strong enough to beat off anyone or anything attacking the sheep. Man needs a shepherd in periods of emotional valleys of death. "Yea, thought I walk through the valley of the shadow of death, I will fear no evil, for Thou art with me. Thy rod and Thy staff they comfort me."

Let me mention one more emotional valley of death. I have saved this particular emotional valley for last because it is one in which all of us spend too much of our time—the valley of worry, the valley of tension. If sheep would worry at any time during their lifetime it should be the time when they are crossing the valley of death in Palestine to get from one feeding ground to another. Suppose I were one of those sheep and wanted to die young with an ulcerated stomach or wind up with a nervous breakdown. Do you know how I would do this? Let me tell you.

My shepherd leads me down into the still waters, but I would worry about getting back up the steep banks of that stream; worry about the water—if it were pure or not; about the dangers that might be awaiting me on the upper banks of the stream; and I would worry over the ability of my shepherd to find another stream later during the day as we shifted to another pasture. I would worry about the grass supply as I grazed in the green valleys and, most of all, my mind would dwell on the valley of death. I would recall every sheep story I had heard about how the wild, vicious dogs pulled this sheep or that sheep from the path; how a weak sheep failed to make the wide jump and fell to its death in the cruel valley below. I would worry about the skill of the shepherd to defend my life when the wolf came upon us in that valley. I would question his loyalty to me and the other sheep.

When I had gotten through with all these worries, I am afraid I would find that I did not have time to put on the fat I needed to withstand the cold nights of the mountains of Palestine, and that I did not have time to grow the soft wool the sheep of Palestine grow, and it would not be very long before I would find myself being sold for lamb chops in the meat markets of Palestine.

"Foolish sheep," you say. He can do nothing about the grass, the water, or even about the wild dogs in the valley of death. He is not even equipped like other animals to defend himself. He is the most helpless of all animals and must look, without reservation, to the shepherd for protection and food. But in doing this, they find peace, happiness, and protection they need to be contented sheep.

David is saying to us, "Oh, foolish man, why be fearful of life? Why drag yourself down to an early grave, an unhappy one at that, by worrying? Do like the sheep do. Turn yourself over to the Good Shepherd. Trust Him completely. He will carry you safely through your emotional valleys of death. But you must commit yourself to Him without reservation. And in trusting Him, you do not—cannot—rely upon self. He has to be the Shepherd of your life." "Yea, though I walk through the valley of the shadow of death, I will fear no evil, for Thou art with me. Thy rod and Thy staff they comfort me. I am the Good Shepherd. The Good Shepherd giveth his life for his sheep."

Taken Aside by Jesus

Taken aside by Jesus,
   To feel the touch of His hand;
To rest awhile in the shadow
   of the Rock in a weary land.

Taken aside by Jesus,
   In the loneliness dark and drear;
Where no other comfort can reach me
   Than His voice to my heart so dear.

Taken aside by Jesus,
　　To be quite alone with Him;
To hear His wonderful tones of love,
　　'Mid the silence and shadows dim.

Taken aside by Jesus,
　　Shall I drink from the desert place
When I hear as I never heard before,
　　And see Him face to face?
　　　　　　　　　—Author Unknown

CHAPTER 11

Beware of the
Spiritual Shadows of Life

In our last chapter, we examined the "Valley of the Shadow of Death" as recorded in the Twenty-Third Psalm by David. We noted that this was a valley outside of Jerusalem and that it had a one-way path through it to sides some fifteen hundred feet above the bottom of the valley. Death lurked on every foot of this four-and-a-half-mile path which led from one feeding ground to another. Wild dogs and other wild animals lived off the prey they snatched off the trail or that fell off the path. Sheep have learned to trust their shepherd as they traveled through this valley, for the shadows of death are everywhere.

David was thinking of himself as he lived, day to day, in the shadows of death in this life. Like a sheep, he had no defense, save that of the staff of His Shepherd. He could not probe each dark shadow overlooking this path, nor could he defend himself against the unexpected rush of a wild animal. If he were to live in serenity and peace, he would have to look to the Good Shepherd of his life, and not to his danger.

We are classifying the valleys of the shadow of death we must pass through in our lives into three categories. In our last chapter, we looked into the emotional valleys of death. In this chapter, we want to look into the spiritual valleys of death we shall pass through from day to day. David said, "Yea, though I walk through the valley of the shadow of death, I will fear no evil, for Thou art with me. Thy rod and Thy staff they comfort me." Jesus once said of the shepherd, "The good shepherd giveth his life for his sheep."

We need to face three facts about this life. One, man will have to live in the presence of certain shadows of death. This is the kind of world that, if one permits his mind to dwell on this fact, life would soon lose its joy for man, and his life would be filled with fears of uncertainties. No one can live at his best under such circumstances. To ignore the fact of these shadows would be an act of folly, for it is impossible to ignore them even if we try. That leads us to another fact. Man needs, and must have, someone or something to help him walk safely through the valleys of the shadow of death. Sheep perished passing through that valley of the shadow of death mentioned in this Psalm. Many died trying to get through without a shepherd.

God did not make man, put him on this earth, and walk off and leave him to survive or perish. Before sin separated the first man and God, God made a daily visit to have communion with man. We have no record of what took place during those daily visits of God with man, but we do know this: Man was not left alone to fight his daily battles without someone to guide him.

The third fact is that God wants to be man's shepherd; to walk with him through all valleys of the shadows of death in this life. No man need try to travel through any valley of death without God as his shepherd. And if man does, he does so by his own choice. We have already seen what happens to man when he attempts to pass through the emotional valley of death without a shepherd. Now let us consider the danger we face when we attempt to pass through the spiritual valley of the shadow of death without a shepherd.

This chapter is addressed to those who profess to be Christians. If a Christian listens to Satan, he will try to make you believe that since you have accepted Christ and have joined the church, you have nothing to worry about. When he gets you lulled to sleep, you find yourself running into problems in your spiritual life. Something happens to shake your faith in God, or in your church. The services of your church seem less interesting, and excuses begin to be made by you for not attending church; for not reading your Bible; for not praying; and for not supporting your church with your presence and your money. David had several such experiences. He cried out one day, "Restore unto me the joy of my salvation." He had found himself in a spiritual death valley, alone, without his shepherd. But what a difference in his words in the Twenty-Third Psalm when he says, "The Lord is my shepherd. Yea, though I walk through the valley of the shadow of death, I will fear no evil, for Thou art with me. Thy rod and Thy staff they comfort me."

Satan knows better than most Christians that he cannot reclaim your soul. When Christ saved you, He gave you a new nature—an eternal nature. The bondage of sin was broken. The sin bondage that would drag one down into an eternal hell is gone forever. Jesus decreed this when He said, "I give unto them eternal life," and again when Paul said, "Nothing can separate us from the love of God, which is in Christ Jesus." Satan knows this, but that does not stop him from trying to rob God of the influence and services of Christians, nor of his attempt to rob the Christian of the spiritual joy of his salvation which is rightfully his as a child of God.

Man passes through three kinds of spiritual valleys. One comes with the physical setbacks of life and from the disappointments of life. Let us take the example of a splendid Christian. He is giving his best in the service of his church. He loses his health, his job, or he suffers great losses in the business world. Quickly, the world says, "See, what did you gain by being a Christian? I am not a Christian and I am better off than you." Satan comes to us and we begin to feel that we have been mistreated by God—that God has let us down. We enter into the shadows of spiritual death. We lose some of the warmth and love we once had for the things of God. We find ourselves in the fault-finders group, sitting with the mourners. We have not reached out and up to grasp the hand of our God when the dark shadows began to close in around us, and we find that we are walking alone.

The Bible does not say that a Christian would never face losses, be exempt from hurts, not be tempted, or never be crippled or killed. Bullets in a war do not seek out only the ungodly; in fact, death seems to strike most often among those who are Christian. Some of the finest Christians I knew overseas were ones that did not come back. I remember once I was returning from the front lines during the Battle of the Bulge with one of my doctors. He was not a Christian, and we were discussing the death of the finest Christian doctor we had. This man turned to me and asked, "You believe in a good God. Please explain to me why that good God would take this fine Christian doctor and not take me instead." My answer to this bitter question? "I do not know the mind of God, nor God's will for all his children, but I do know that this man was ready to meet God, and that death for the Christian is the most wonderful thing that can happen to him. Also, God could have chosen him instead of you because you were not prepared to meet God at this time, and would have ended up, not in heaven, but in hell."

Physical losses and life's disappointments are but spiritual valleys we must pass through in this world, and if one walks close to the Good Shepherd, one can pass through them safely into greener valleys. "Yea, though I walk through the valley of the shadow of death, I will fear no evil, for Thou art with me. Thy rod and Thy staff they comfort me." This is one of the differences between the Christian and the non-Christian. One has a shepherd who walks with him through the spiritual valleys of the shadow of death, and the other must walk into and through such shadows without the companionship of the Good Shepherd.

Christians are sometimes thrust into spiritual valleys of the shadows of death by someone shattering one's faith in that individual. This is especially true among Christians who hold positions of trust and influence in their church and community. Sons and daughters have had their lives thrust into the darkest of all spiritual shadows by their parents failing to live up to the ideals and principles of Christ. Church members, adrift in the world from their church, often point back to some deacon, elder, minister, bishop, or Sunday School teacher who broke faith with their ideals and principles.

Paul had something to say about this in his letters to the Christians at Corinth. He spoke first to the strong Christians, admonishing them not to use their liberties just because they were strong. Paul said the strong Christian should consider the weaker Christian who might be watching him as an example, and also act as his earthly guide. But on the other hand, Paul cautioned the weaker Christian not to depend upon what he saw in another, and not to let himself lean upon anyone, but to lean upon Christ. Man will fail, but Christ—never.

A woman took me to task one day when her child presented himself for church membership. She did not want the child to be baptized in our church, but she did want the boy to be baptized and live a Christian life. When I pressed her for the reason why she did not want him baptized in our church she said that years ago, when she was a young lady, somebody in the church had hurt her feelings. She had nursed that hurt all these years. It did no good to remind her that among our present membership, numbering nearly two thousand, few, if any of the present membership, were members of the church when she had been hurt, but this did not make any difference. She had walked to that valley of spiritual death alone. She did not take her shepherd with her, and its shadows had completely covered her life all those years. I have not seen the mother or the boy, to my knowledge, since that morning. What a price to pay for the mistake of another. Her son will also share in the payment of her debt.

Nowhere in the New Testament will you find that we are to

look to others for our excuses for wrong. Jesus does say, however, that we are to look to Him for all our needs.

One of the greatest disappointments, if not *the* greatest earthly disappointment to Jesus, must have been the denial of his most devout disciple, Peter. In the hour Jesus needed encouragement the most, Peter denied his Lord. Another disciple, his treasurer Judas, sold him for thirty pieces of silver. My greatest hurts in the ministry have not come from outside of my church, but from men I loved most in my churches. If Jesus had looked to his disciples, he would have left this world keenly disappointed and fearful for the success of His Kingdom on earth. Instead, He looked to the power of the Holy Spirit and the power of God's love for the success of his kingdom. Ministers are more often disappointed in their people than the people in their ministers. And the reason why few leave the ministry is that early in their ministry, they have learned to look for the hand of Jesus, and not of man, to guide them as they travel through dark spiritual valleys of death. "Thy rod and Thy staff they comfort me."

A third valley that takes its toll of God's children is the valley of the shadow of personal failures of Christians, themselves. They enter into God's kingdom with all the enthusiasm of children entering into a picnic. They are sincere, and want to make a success of their Christian lives. They find themselves failing to measure up to the standards they have set for themselves. They find themselves being defeated by temptation. They cannot carry a job through successfully, and so they turn and run from the presence of their failures. Some run to a different church; some to a different denomination. Changing environment seems to them the answer to their failures. But deep down in their own hearts they know that failure is within, although they will not face up to it themselves, and they blame others for these failures.

One of the meanest men I knew in the Army was a man who was superintendent of a Sunday School at one time. His whole Christian life was a failure during the three-year period I knew him. Not only was he lost to the service of Christ, but his life became a stumbling block to all those with whom he came into contact.

Failures are common in religion. Ministers have their share, let me assure you. Failures come many times because we are not prepared to do the job we want to do. Many times we think that we are stronger spiritually than we really are to withstand temptation, and when we are overcome by temptation, we lose confidence in ourselves, and turn and run from God. The Bible says that all who are born into God's kingdom come in as babies, and it does not matter at what age we are saved and join the church. We need to grow into manhood and womanhood in Christ in a normal way. No one in his right mind would expect a baby to do a man's work, nor resist a mansized effort to toss him out of the crib. God does not expect more of us. What He does expect of all of us is that we let Him be our shepherd at all times, and when we do this we will have Him at our side, even amid the spiritual valleys of the shadow of death. "Yea, though I walk through the valley of the shadow of death, I will fear no evil, for Thou art with me. Thy rod and Thy staff they comfort me."

Remember this when you find yourself in the spiritual shadows that fall upon your life—you have the Good Shepherd by your side, ready to carry you through, and there can be no fear for His sheep when He is near.

I do not think God has meant
　　For shadows to be fearsome things.
Else He would not have given us
　　The shadows of His wings.
Nor would His tall trees by the way
　　Trace out a cool, sweet place
Where weary travelers may pause
　　To find His soothing grace.

Nor would the shadows of the night
   Enfold us in that tranquil rest
That falls upon the sleeping babe
   Rocked on its mother's breast.
And though the shadows over life
   May seem to creep apace,
Behind the darkest ones of them
   Is His assuring face.

                —Mrs. C. A. Mackay

CHAPTER 12

A Shepherd for the
Valley of Physical Death

A Southern Christian woman, while dying, imagined in her delirium that she was riding in her carriage with her faithful Negro servant in the driver's seat. "Is David driving?" she asked. "There is no danger if David is driving."

"No, no, Missus," replied the weeping Negro at her side. "Poor David can't drive now. De Lord has hold of de lines."

This humble servant spoke the truth for all ages. The Lord of Life holds the lines and guides his children safely through the gate of death into the Paradise of God.

"The Lord is my shepherd, I shall not want. He maketh me to lie down in green pastures. He leadeth me beside the still waters. He restoreth my soul. . . . Yea, though I walk through the valley of the shadow of death, I will fear no evil for Thou art with me. Thy rod and Thy staff they comfort me." In the last two chapters, we have learned of the valleys of emotional and spiritual death through which man walks as he lives his life. In our study of this Psalm, we have noted that David based each line, each thought, upon some real experience he had as a shepherd of sheep. We already noted that the "valley of the shadow of death" was actually a valley of death for sheep just outside the city of Jerusalem, which had a very narrow path leading through it. Wild animals preyed upon each flock that passed through this valley to reach better feeding grounds. Sheep without a shepherd had little chance of getting through safely, but a good shepherd carried every one of his sheep through it without loss. He would

fight off the wild beasts with his staff and rod, knocking the at-
tacker off the narrow path.

Every man has to pass through a physical valley of death. To
one, it will actually be a valley of death, but to another it will
be merely a valley of death shadows. All living things on this
earth will end up in a physical death. None can escape it. It
matters not how short or how long one does live—death is at the
end of every life. Death is the most ignored obvious fact known
to man. We all try to close our minds to it, and when it strikes
near us, we are surprised and shocked by its sudden appearance.
Man has never gotten used to the idea of death, nor has he been
able to adjust himself to the idea, so he refuses to think about it.

Death for the Christian is nothing more than a door to a better life. It is the door to all the hidden, unrealized dreams, am-
bitions, and longed-for joys of the soul. It is the only entrance to
eternity with God. To the Christian, it becomes merely a shadow
across the path of life as he goes from a lower level of life to a
higher one. But on the other hand, to one without a shepherd,
death is a place of horrible experiences, filled with dangers and
hopelessness.

The word "death" means separation. In and by death, man is
separated from his loved ones on earth. Death does not mean that
this state is final, for all Christians will be together with God at
the end of this earthly life. To such persons, death is merely a
shadow we pass through to await the coming of the Lord. "Yea,
though I walk through the valley of the shadow of death, I will
fear no evil." Thus, the sheep feel the shadows of death all
around them; they can smell the danger of a hungry lion, but
these things are hidden in the shadows, and the sheep knows
that between himself and that danger, the shepherd stands with
his rod and staff.

I said that death comes to all, the good and the bad, the Christian and the non-Christian. To the Christian, death is merely a
shadow, but to the non-Christian—to the shepherdless—death be-

comes an eternal separation. It becomes a physical separation from all that is good, decent, fine, and Godly. Death becomes a door of hopelessness and helplessness. It is a final act of destruction. It is a land of no return, and a land of no reunions. Refusal to think on these facts or a denial of them in your own heart does not change them. A trip to any cemetery will convince you of the fact of death and, if you should make such a trip, look around that cemetery and tell yourself, "within the next fifty or seventy-five years I, too, will be in a grave just like these."

I once read a sad story of a lovely girl in her late teens. She lay dying amid all the luxury that money could buy. Medical science had done its best to save her young life, but without success. As she faced the dark shadows of death, she looked up into her mother's face and said a very strange thing. She said, "Mother, you have been a wonderful mother to me; have given me everything that money could buy and that I wanted. You taught me how to develop a good personality, to dance, to carry on a good conversation with people in all walks of life. You have taught me all the graces of good living, but now when I come face to face with the reality of death, I find that you have not taught me the most important thing in my life. I do not know how to face this experience. I do not know how to face death. Oh, mother, you did not teach me how to die." And with these words, she died without a shepherd to guide her through the valley of the shadow of death. No one is prepared to live until he is prepared to die. And no one is prepared to live or die until he has found the Good Shepherd. "The Lord is my Shepherd, I shall not want. . . . Yea, though I walk through the valley of the shadow of death, I will fear no evil, for Thou art with me. Thy rod and Thy staff they comfort me." Death valley is at the end of every life. It is either a valley made up only of shadows, or it is a valley of death. 'Tis the shepherd that makes the difference; but, oh, what a difference He makes to the traveler as he walks through the valley of the shadow of death.

This second thought is addressed only to the Christian; to the ones who have found the Good Shepherd and to those who are living within his sheepfold. David wrote these words just for you. "The Lord is my shepherd, I shall not want. . . . Yea, though I walk through the valley of the shadow of death, I will fear no evil, for Thou art with me. Thy rod and Thy staff they comfort me." Notice the words, "I will fear no evil." If you are a Christian and live in fear of death, you are sinning against yourself and against God. Sheep travel through their valleys of death without fear, for they trust their shepherd. 'Tis the sheep that lose their faith in their shepherd to provide for their needs that forsake the flock; and in forsaking the shepherd, they find an early death at the will of other animals for they cannot defend themselves. 'Tis the impatient sheep, who will not wait for the flock and his shepherd and dashes on ahead, who is caught by the lion or wolf.

A Christian should not fear the dark, mysterious clouds of death. He can do nothing about them, and should not, for this is the job of his Shepherd. It was Mark Twain who said, "Man worries most about the things that never happen, and about the things he can do nothing about." The Christian has no reason to worry about death. It can never happen to him. Remembering the meaning of the word "separation," the Christian is never separated from his Shepherd—from his God. As he enters the shadows of the thing we call death, he finds Christ there to carry him across. Jesus said, "Lo, I am with you always, and will be with you to the end of the ages." These were the last words spoken to men by the human voice of Jesus. They still stand.

The shepherdless, the non-Christian, ought never to forget the fact of death, but the Christian should give little thought to it. He has nothing to fear from anything he might find behind the curtain of physical death. A child of God has nothing to fear as long as he is in the presence of God, and death cannot, will not, separate us from our Good Shepherd.

What is fear? We can define fear as a projection of ourselves into a future situation which creates a negative emotion in our present lives. One will not be afraid and will lose his fears when he is acting upon the object, or is doing something about the thing he fears. Let us illustrate this. Suppose a boy is about to take an examination. He has studied diligently, but he is not sure of the examination. This particular one determines whether or not he will graduate. As he thinks about this examination, he projects himself into taking and failing of the exam. But when he really sits down to take the examination, he becomes so busy writing out and working out the answers that he finds himself calm and without fear. He arises from his work and says, "Gee, it wasn't as hard or as bad as I thought it was going to be." Anyone who has ever played football or some other sport knows the tightness and tension he feels before the kickoff comes or before the game starts. But when the whistle blows, and that first contact with the opponent is made, this fear is gone.

A lot of Christians are afraid to die. They know that they are saved; that Christ is their shepherd in a very real sense. But death still holds its fear for them. They have yet to learn one of the important laws of God's grace. Here it is. Learn this law, and it will wipe out many fears from your life. *God never gives His grace to any child of His until that child needs that grace.* Grace is not something you can keep in the deep freeze, but it is like the manna God provided for the Children of Israel while they were wandering in the wilderness. You will recall that this bread would not keep more than twenty-four hours. They had to consume each day's supply that day. They learned that on each morrow, God would give them food for that particular day. God gives to each of us just enough grace for this day—not enough for tomorrow. If we try to reach out into the tomorrow for grace, we find not the grace of God out there, but we will find that this grace has become a thing called worry. We are to live one day at a time, and leave the future to our God—to our

Shepherd. This is true about the valleys of the shadow of death. We do not have the grace today to die ten years from now. We do not have the grace now to die an hour from now. God does not promise to give us dying grace during living days. But when the time comes when we need dying grace, we will find his supply is more than adequate and abundant for that occasion.

Now for one final thought. It is not important when or where we die, for we have little control over this, but it is very important to know that when death comes stalking into our lives—announced or unannounced—it will never find us unprepared or alone, for we have the Good Shepherd with us and He is our preparation. "Yea, though I walk through the valley of the shadow of death I will fear no evil, for Thou art with me. Thy rod and Thy staff they comfort me." This word "comfort" does not mean to soothe the feelings with gentle caresses, or with love taps, nor does it mean a sweet, soft embrace. It means that this staff is long enough to reach out and catch that sheep about to slip off the path into the blackness of the valley below. It means that this rod is strong enough to deal death to any animal attacking the sheep. It means that the shepherd is never out of staff-reach or rod-reach of his sheep as long as they are in any danger. Sheep were sometimes bruised in body by the staff of their shepherd, but they did not fear it, for in the hands of their shepherd that loved them, they knew it was a means for him to protect them from their carelessness or from the danger of wild animals as they traveled through the valley of the shadow of death.

Physical death comes in many forms. It might come through long periods of great suffering, even for a Christian. It can come without pain, by the stopping of the heart, or by accident. Man cannot know the mind of God, but our happiness does not rest in our ability to discern the mind of God, but comes to the sheep in their knowing the shepherd. If we know God, through Christ, this brings its own happiness. God's staff might have to bruise us occasionally, but we know that at the other end of that staff is one who loves us and is concerned with our safe arrival in heaven to be with Him through all the ages to come. How can one measure the bruises of this life in the light of an eternity with God!

We might not be able to understand the way, nor even the direction we are traveling, but if we know that we are walking beside the Good Shepherd, what does it matter if we are walking north or south, east or west, for being with Him brings its own reward.

I say again, the Christian has nothing to fear from death. We see only its shadows, for we died when we came to Christ, and there is no other death in our future—only shadows, with Christ standing and walking between us and these shadows. "The Lord is my shepherd, I shall not want. . . . Yea, though I walk through the valley of the shadow of death, I will fear no evil, for Thou art with me. Thy rod and Thy staff they comfort me." And we can say with this one . . .

> The Master will knock at my door some night,
>   And there in the silence hushed and dim
> Will wait for my coming with lamps alight
>   To open immediately to Him.
>
> If this is the only foretold
>   Of all my future, then I pray
> That quietly watchful I may hold
>   The key of a golden faith each day.
>
> Fast shut in my grasp, that, when I hear
>   His steps, be it at dawn or midnight dim,
> Straightway may I rise without a fear,
>   And open immediately to Him

So death has lost its terrors;
    How can we fear it now?
Its face, once grim, now leads to Him
    At whose command we bow.

His presence makes us happy;
    His service our delight,
The many mansions gleam and glow,
    The Saints and Souls invite.

        —MARGARET L. PRESTON

CHAPTER 13

Peace from Power

"I will fear no evil, for Thou art with me. Thy rod and Thy staff they comfort me." This rod of the shepherd was his tool of war. It was his weapon of defense and offense. This was a wooden stick hardened with pitch, with the strength and texture of iron. It was an effective weapon in the hands of a strong man. The sheep of Palestine had many enemies. They lived in a vicious environment. A careless shepherd could lose his flock in a short time. His job was not only to find and select the best pastures and water for his sheep, but to defend his sheep with his own life.

"I am the door [of the sheep]. By me if any man enter in, he shall be saved, and shall go in and out, and find pasture." "The thief cometh not but for to steal, and to kill and to destroy. But I am come that they might have life, and that they might have it more abundantly. I am the Good Shepherd. The Good Shepherd giveth his life for his sheep. But he that is an hireling, and not the shepherd, seeth the wolf coming, and leaveth the sheep, and fleeth. And the wolf catcheth the sheep, and scattereth them. The hireling fleeth because he is a hireling, and careth not for the sheep. I am the Good Shepherd, and I know my sheep and am known of mine. As the Father knoweth me, even so know I the Father, and I lay down my life for my sheep." (John 10:9-15).

There is an often used phrase in sports—"leading from strength." The sheep of God's flock "lead from strength"—live by the strength of God. Paul's statement, "I can do all things through Christ Jesus who strengthens me" was a shout of confidence in his ability to accomplish the impossible for God. He knew his power to achieve rested in God's willingness to share His great power with him.

I swam ashore on D Day in Sicily, and I climbed to the hill overlooking our landing beaches. I looked down on an Armada of American warships of every description, from landing craft to battleships. I knew within myself that no human power on earth could defeat us or drive us off that island. We "led from strength." We had the manpower and the fire power to achieve victory over our enemy—and we did accomplish this within thirty days.

David's sheep had seen the strength of David demonstrated as he drove off the wild vicious animals that would have destroyed his flock. They had seen the destructive power of David's rod as it destroyed the would-be destroyer. They feared it not for it was never used against the sheep; only against their enemy. "Thy rod and Thy staff they comfort me." Peace from power.

Peace comes from the abundance of our supplies. We were driving through France on our way to an unmanned Germany defense, the West Wall. There was little between us and Berlin at the time we broke out of the Normandy beachhead. Most of the Germans were smashed behind us or were fighting in Russia. We were within days of ending World War II.

Then we received orders to stop our drive. We had depleted our supplies. We did not have enough supplies to carry us all the way to Berlin. Just one ship of ammunition and one tanker of fuel for our tanks and trucks was all we needed. We lacked an abundance of supplies needed for a quick charge for victory. By the time we had been resupplied, Germans had withdrawn troops from Russia, manned its western fortifications, and were ready for us. One year later we finished our conquest of the German army. More than fifty thousand American graves had been dug and filled. These graves should not have been necessary.

The Christian should, and can, live in peace with himself for he knows God can, and does, supply all he needs out of the abundance of God. When one becomes a child of God through faith in Christ Jesus, he is not only given salvation, but the key to God's storehouse from whence will come the supplies to satisfy all his earthly needs! Peace from power—unlimited, abundant power.

Peace comes through the sheep's close relationship to this power—the shepherd. "Thou art with me. Thy rod and Thy staff they comfort me." Sheep live in a small, limited world. A few small valleys and hills is all the world they ever see in their lifetime. Their shepherd is their only contact with the world beyond those hills. He is their God, guardian, and deliverer. He lives with them throughout their lifetime. He is all they know, but to know him and his power satisfies all their needs.

Jesus used the figures of speech "shepherd," "sheep," and "flock," deliberately. The people of his day knew exactly what he meant by these words, "I am the Good Shepherd." The sheep belong to the good shepherd. They were his. He was hired to watch over his flock of sheep.

Jesus contrasted this relationship to his own by pointing out the difference between the Good Shepherd and the hireling—one who receives wages from an owner of sheep to tend his sheep by saying, "I am the Good Shepherd. The Good Shepherd giveth his life for his sheep." This Jesus did on the Cross of Calvary.

Now the contrast of shepherds: "But he that is a hireling, and not the shepherd, whose own they are not, seeth the wolf coming, and leaveth the sheep and fleeth: and the wolf catcheth them and scattereth the sheep. The hireling fleeth because he is a hireling, and careth not for the sheep. I am the Good Shepherd and know my sheep, and am known of mine. As the Father knoweth me, even so know I the Father: and I lay down my life for my sheep." (John 10:11-15).

Peace from power. The sheep might be docile and helpless to defend themselves from unknown powers, but the shepherd is powerful and has sufficient supplies and power to satisfy all their needs.

CHAPTER 14

Peace from Pain

Men have some characteristics of sheep. One of these is the need for pain in conditioning man to accept the bitter things of life. No one likes to suffer pain—it matters not if it is emotional pain, spiritual pain, or physical pain. Man's tolerance of pain is very low. The female of the human race seems to have a higher tolerance of pain than her counterpart, the male. But neither likes pain and will do much to avoid it. God uses pain under certain circumstances in dealing with men. God has to use pain as a teaching experience for many of his own—his sheep. He does not like to use pain, but we often leave God with no other choice.

Many years ago I read a story about a shepherd that left an imprint upon my mind that time has not been able to erase. It seemed that this shepherd had one sheep that was an iconoclast—it would not conform to the rules of the flock. He was constantly wandering away from the other sheep and seemed to lose all sense of danger that surrounded him. His shepherd constantly had to keep his eye on him. On a certain day, this independent sheep left the flock and found himself alone on a ledge just below the trail. He could not find his way off this ledge. It had been very easy for him to jump down to the ledge early that morning, but he could not jump high enough to get off the ledge when he decided to find his way back to the other sheep. The shepherd heard his frightened cry and soon located him below the path on the ledge. After thinking over the plight of the sheep, the shepherd decided to let him remain where he was until he had eaten all the grass on the ledge. A few days later, the shepherd returned for his sheep. By this time the sheep was weak from lack of food and water. The shepherd picked him up, placed him on his shoulders, refreshed him with water and grass, and returned him to the flock. When asked about the treatment of this wayward sheep, the shepherd explained, "He had to learn through pain; to learn that it was better to remain with the shepherd and other sheep than to go it alone. That sheep had to learn the hard way. He would not have learned any other way."

The rod and staff of the shepherd could, and did, inflict pain upon some of his sheep. But it was the pain of peace; of security and of safety—not pain of punishment. "I will fear no evil, for Thou art with me. Thy rod and Thy staff they comfort me." Oh, yes, they do cause me pain, but it is far better to suffer pain that saves, than no pain and die. God gives pain to warn us that we are nearing the edge of life. The long staff of the shepherd reaches out to the sheep getting too near the edge of the trail winding through the valley of the shadow of death. If the sheep does not respond to the gentle pressure of the shepherd's staff, he can expect greater pain. The life of that sheep is at stake. A little pain is better than death lurking just off the trail.

Nature tries to use the same technique with us. We drive ourselves almost to a point of physical exhaustion, ignoring all God's attempts to warn us, and when we push ourselves over the brink, we exclaim, "How did this happen to me?" It happened because we ignored the gentle staff of God.

During World War II, I served thirty-three months in combat. I lived with my medical staff twenty-four hours a day. I watched strong, healthy, young men deteriorate before my eyes. An expression was coined to explain this phenomenon. It was called "shell shock." This was a misnomer. Our medical commander was a psychiatrist from New York City. I asked him to explain what happened to these men. I had majored for my doctorate in the field of psychology. I wanted a medical reason for what I saw happening to physically strong men. His explanation was simple: the human nervous system was built to endure stress and strain over a life time (seventy years), but if these stresses became too strong to bear within too short a span of time, nature will protect itself by short-circuiting the nervous system. Man reverts back to the basic animal instincts to protect himself. This can best be illustrated with a common rubber band. Nature built into rubber an elastic quality. You can pull a rubber band, release it, and it will return to its normal size and position, but if you pull it too far or too often, it will break. God uses His staff to keep us from breaking ourselves.

These gentle reminders come from God in many ways. They come in the form of physical reminders that we are going too far too quickly for our own safety. I am the director of a great hospital. The recovery of cardiac patients brought to us is ten times the average of other hospitals in the United States. If I were to have a heart attack, I would rather be in my hospital than any place in the United States. A cliché among our internists—heart specialists—is, "You are lucky if your first heart attack does not kill you." Why? Is this true? And it is. You see, once you survive your first heart attack, you learn to listen to your body when it signals you of certain dangers. If you listen and obey, your chances of dying of other diseases is greater than dying of a heart attack.

The laws of God are not broken by man. Men are broken by these laws. If I should decide that I am going to break the laws of gravity, and I climb to the top of the Washington Monument and jump off, I will be broken by this law. And the law of gravity continues on its unbroken pattern—either as a service to man or to destroy man. We can use this law to fly an airplane or destroy the mountain climber who loses his footing.

God's staff is to comfort us and to give us peace and security. "I will fear no evil, for Thou art with me. Thy rod and Thy staff they comfort me." Surgeons, every day, cause great pain to their patients as they cut into the human body to remove diseased organs, foreign bodies that would kill, and correct broken bones so that they might heal correctly—all this at great pain to their patients. Is this an act of punishment or of peace? Jesus was not called the Great Physician without cause. He did heal the sick, raise the dead, and perform many miracles. But we must remind ourselves that even He, the Holy One of God, could and did heal only the ones who came to Him. Those he healed during His lifetime did not make a dent—an impression—on the sick population of the world. This is not a judgment of Him, but a judgment upon those whom he came to "seek and to save." They refused to accept his pain of peace.

Pain—is it for punishment or for peace? The answer rests with you.

CHAPTER 15

It Is Not Where You Eat
But What You Eat

"The Lord is my shepherd . . . Thou preparest a table before me in the presence of mine enemies." In the Orient, the shepherd is more than a keeper of sheep. Not only has he the responsibility of protecting his sheep from outside dangers, he also must protect his sheep from themselves. In the grazing fields each spring of the year, poisonous plants spring up. The shepherd has to know how to recognize such plants and then grub them out before his sheep can feed in that pasture. He grubs out such plants and then places them upon stone pyres, or altars, built by shepherds before him, out of reach of his sheep. The plants are left to dry out until they can be burned. The sheep can see these drying plants and also smell them, but they cannot be harmed by them. David was thinking of this protective act of the shepherd when he penned the line in this Psalm, "Thou preparest a table before me in the presence of mine enemies." The sheep eat and graze in the presence of the plants, their enemy, without fear, for that which would kill them has been placed out of their reach by their shepherd.

This same thought is carried over in the New Testament in the words spoken by Jesus in the sixth chapter of John's Gospel, verses forty-seven to fifty-one: "I am the bread of life. Your fathers did eat manna in the wilderness and are dead. This is the bread which cometh down from heaven that a man may eat thereof, and not die. I am the living bread which came down from heaven; if any man eat of this bread, he shall live forever;

and the bread that I give is my flesh, which I will give for the life of the world."

Satan has planted poisonous weeds in God's earthly garden. The word of God, the Bible, was given to us to help us recognize such weeds and, thus, we can avoid eating them. Satan strikes us through the God-given instinct we possess. These mental, spiritual, and physical instincts are not evil until we turn them over to be used by Satan. The non-Christian is without the Spirit of God in making such determinations. The Christian has the Spirit of God to assist him to make them. We are like the sheep with a good shepherd; we can live in the world and not be destroyed by the world. God does, through His Son, prepare for us daily a table in the presence of our enemy, but there is one important difference between sheep and man: the sheep cannot reach up and eat that which has been placed on the pyres for drying—that which would harm him. But man can reach up and over the arms of God and eat that which he should not. This is to sin against the revealed knowledge of God. The sinner might not know the good from the bad, but the Christian does know, or can know if he wishes to know. We have God's divine book of spiritual botany to identify the plants of sin, and what is more, we have the Divine teacher of God—the Holy Spirit—to guide us as we study this divine book, the Bible. In the next three chapters we are going to study the poisonous plants placed in God's garden to destroy man, and also to point out what Christ has done about these plants.

"The Lord is my shepherd . . . Thou preparest a table before me in the presence of mine enemies." Christ, the Christian's Shepherd, can be trusted to remove the plants which are dangerous in the moral grazing grounds of man. Satan tries—and is more than successful in these attempts—to booby-trap our morals. I served three years with combat engineers during World War II. Our principal job was to remove enemy mines and booby traps so that our soldiers could get through to the enemy or make safe the areas captured from the enemy. The Germans were very skillful in laying mines and in booby-trapping. They would retreat from a town and leave death for the unsuspecting, in many forms. It might be a picture hanging at an angle on the wall of a home; a chair to be placed on its feet; a door to be opened; a car left on the street. A thousand soldiers lost their lives through these traps.

Have you heard it said, "When in Rome, do as the Romans do?" "Don't be a wet blanket." "Everybody is doing it, it must be alright." These are a few of the triggers that explode Satan's moral booby traps. They are but blossoms on the poisonous weeds in the moral garden of man. In these pages we shall look at three dangerous weeds we must avoid; weeds that will be plucked out by our Shepherd if we will let him do it.

In the sacred garden of marriage, Satan has planted the poisonous weed of divorce, and the free-love attitude. The Bible says, "What God has joined together, let no man put asunder." This means either party of the marriage, or someone outside of that marriage. God's plan for one man for one woman, and one woman for one man is the only safe plan for the human race.

No nation in the world has the delinquent problem we have in America, and yet, no nation offers its youth more in the material world, in the educational sphere, or in the spiritual sense. Yet more crimes—major crimes—are committed by young people under the age of twenty-one, than above that age. More unhappiness stems from our American homes than from any other source. Why? The answer is to be found in the poison weeds of free-love and divorce. Children reared in homes that have divorce courts for the back door of their homes have a poor chance to make well-balanced adults. They have two strikes on them as they live in these American cities where the poisonous weeds are growing faster than the sweet, nourishing green grass. In many American cities there are as many divorces as there are marriages.

This seed is planted before such marriages take place. God said that a man and woman should be made one in His sight when the two come together through the medium of love, a love that is not merely the passion of sexes. Real love is deeper than mere physical attraction. Real love will not enter into marriage with an eye on the divorce courts if all does not go well. The divorce seeds we are planting with such abandonment in America will someday be the poison that will help destroy America. You cannot destroy the homes of America without destroying the country itself.

Marriage is a sacred institution. It should be approached with reverence. God must be a partner to it if that marriage is to be sure of succeeding. Jesus used the figure or example of marriage to explain His great love and respect for the church.

The frightening thing about this weed is that our churches have made this weed a respectable member of society by excusing those who use it for an easy way out of a bad bargain. We are afraid to take the Biblical stand against those who practice it. We are not trying to uproot this plant, but to remove the poison from it because we like its beauty.

The Bible teaches that there is only one ground for a divorce —the ground of adultery by either member of the marriage. The innocent party is free to divorce and remarry. There is no sin to the innocent party in such a divorce or remarriage. But this is not true for the guilty party. He lives in sin if he or she should remarry, and the Bible says that the one who marries the guilty party also sins. God's plan is for one man and one woman for one marriage until death separates them. Satan has altered this plan to read, "One man for one woman, one at a time, and the change can be made on any condition." He would also justify this by saying, "Man has a right to be happy, and if he makes a mistake in marriage, he ought to have the right to correct it." God calls this sin. Also, an unbiased study of divorce records will show that divorce begets divorce. One divorce leads to another, and children of divorced parents divorce more often than children from nondivorced parents. God's saying a thing is wrong does not make it wrong—but God says a thing is wrong because it *is* wrong. God's strict law of marriage is that way. Know His plan is best for man's own happiness and good. Let me say another word about this subject. There is no difference between the words "divorce" and "annulment," as used by some churches to avoid the ugly word "divorce." Jesus took the people to task about this practice of juggling words to appease their religious consciences when he said that Moses gave them writs of separation because their hearts were spiritually hard, but this did not change the situation in the eyes of God.

Satan plants poison weeds amid the fields of pleasure for God's children. There are many forms of wholesome pleasure a Christian can indulge in without harm. God wants man to be happy on this earth and to enjoy life. Jesus himself was criticized quite severely because he enjoyed certain pleasures. They said that he ate with the wrong crowd, ate too much, got too much joy from life, did not cry enough, was too much of a mixer, and on and on they went.

Satan plants two varieties of seed in this garden. The seed of no pleasure at all—a very unattractive flower and one without fragrance, beauty, or desirability. Its flowers can be described as "longfaceness," "grimness," "smilelessness," and a life that says, "I am not happy in my religion and you ought not to be either." The idea behind this flower is that the more we suffer on this earth, the greater our joys will be on the other side of death. The danger of this plant is what it does to young people who want to come into the garden of God—want to become a sheep of the Master, but are forced to make decisions against all God-given instincts for the joys of life because of the influence of these negative people, these unattractive flowers without beauty, fragrance, or desirability.

The other extreme is the seed of pleasure for pleasure's sake.

We use pleasure to run away from life's responsibilities, to cover up a guilty conscience, or we become slaves to pleasure itself. Such weeds in our lives will kill our spiritual lives, cause us to lose our spiritual glow and power, and in the end, leave us with wasted lives.

The Bible is quite clear on many moral issues. Man cannot play the game according to the plan of the world. The Christian will have to control all his instincts and direct them into channels of usefulness for himself, others, and his God if he is to be happy.

To the sheep of David's time, a poison weed looked and smelled like any other kind of plant, but if the shepherd placed it out of his reach, he was to leave it alone. After all, the plants that the shepherd removed from the pastures were few in number compared to the many that were left.

Satan would have us believe that all the pleasures of life are evil, and that, if one becomes a Christian, he has to give them all up. He will tell young Christians not to give God their lives in dedicated service, for to do so means giving up every form of pleasure. When I surrendered to full-time Christian service as a young man, I really felt sorry for myself for the first few weeks, for I had learned to enjoy life to the fullest. One of the many wonderful things I have learned in the service of my Saviour is the great joy which has been mine. I feel sorry for anyone who has not learned this. One does not really know what real happiness is until he is living within the will of the Lord for his life.

The third pasture Satan tries to ruin for man with his poison weeds is in the area of the physical needs of the body. The Bible says that the body is the temple for the Spirit of God, and that we are to keep it as a fit temple for this Spirit of God. God has placed into the framework of the human body certain desires, or instincts. Satan plays upon these to destroy the beauty of God's earthly temples. The sex drive, which is in all normal bodies, is not an evil thing, but only becomes so when given over to the use of Satan. God made man and woman to attract each other. It is not good for man to live alone, nor for woman. Satan enters into this garden and turns this drive into sin outside of marriage and in broken marriages. Today we use the sex drive to sell anything and everything from razor blades to automobiles. We see the sinful use of this holy thing peering from every magazine, newspaper, and from the T.V. screens and movie houses of America.

Satan takes the normal appetites of man for food and drink and creates drunkards and gluttons out of millions. In America we are drinking our nation into the gutters of the world. There is a greater increase in women drinkers in America than among men. The end is not yet in sight toward this trend. It is only in recent years we have learned that smoking is a killer of the body. Now it is the doctors, and not the ministers, who are urging America to give up the smoking habit.

Our bodies are temples of God. God expects us to have good, clean, strong bodies. Those of us who inherited disease-free bodies from Christian parents owe as much to our yet unborn generations. Satan would have it otherwise, saying to young people, "You are young but once. Get the most from your beautiful, young lives; you will have time to obey God when you are too old to enjoy life." Do not believe him. This is another booby-trap to destroy something which is good.

"The Lord is my shepherd . . . Thou preparest a table before me in the presence of mine enemies." Christ does this for us. He does pluck out those things for us that will hurt or destroy us, but we ought to be like the sheep of David's fold and not try to reach up and eat that which has been removed. If we will let Him be our Shepherd, we can and will accept the pastures into which He leads us. They will be cleaned of danger, and we can eat with safety.

Suppose you were very thirsty and came upon two streams. You knew that one held pure, wholesome water, and the other contained polluted water. From which stream would you drink? Two ways of life are offered to men—one by God and the other by Satan. One is not only a safe way, but one of supreme happiness. The other is questionable, uncertain, and dangerous. Which should be the way chosen by man? Which one have you chosen?

Lord, Touch Me with Splendor

Lord, touch with splendor all our thoughts,
 That nothing commonplace may be,
But all with loveliness inwrought
 Since all things are in Thee.
Grant every task shall shine with light
 And nothing be too small to show
Thy glory shining day and night
 In all the ways we go.

Lord, touch with splendor all our thoughts,
 For nothing is that is not Thine,
So let our hearts by Thee be taught
 To see Thy pure design
In common things like daily bread
 And holy things like evening prayer;
Lord, touch with splendor all our thoughts,
 For Thou art everywhere.
   —ELENOR HALBROOK ZIMMERMAN
   (*Daily Word*)

CHAPTER 16

Contaminated Food Can Kill

When I was a small boy, the most satisfying time of the day to me was just before supper time. As a rule, we children would be playing around the backyard at this period of the day. We could hear mother in the kitchen busy about her preparation of the evening meal. Fragrant odors would start drifting out of the kitchen to us. Mother was a wonderful cook, as all mothers are to hungry, growing, healthy boys, and from her kitchen came tantalizing odors. We were not permitted to go into the kitchen or dining room until the meal was on the table, and this only added a keener edge to our appetites. These childhood memories still have their meaning to me as this time of day approaches.

"Thou preparest a table before me in the presence of mine enemies." We saw in the previous chapter that David was referring to the preparation made by the shepherd before he led his sheep into a new pasture each spring. He would go ahead of them and grub out all poisonous weeds in each pasture. He would place them on pyres, stone tables made of native rock, out of reach of the sheep. The same tables were used by shepherds year after year. These poisonous weeds would dry, then the shepherd would burn them. In the meantime, the sheep could graze in the pasture without danger, although he grazed in the presence of the poisonous weeds—his natural enemy.

Satan has planted, and continues to plant, poisonous weeds in man's moral pastures. We dealt with this phrase in the last chapter. In this chapter, we will consider the poisonous weeds Satan plants in the garden of the laws and philosophies of our lives. Everyone of us lives by some fixed law or philosophy. Man is never happy until he has freedom, but he cannot and will not be content until he finds some fixed law, pattern, or philosophy by which he forces himself to live. Call it what you will, man must have a fixed pattern of life to enjoy life. It gives him a sense of freedom acting as a boundary in which he can move around with a sense of freedom. He must use this rule of thumb by which he can measure his success or failure in business, pleasure, or religion. For convenience and clarity, let us group all of these into three sets of laws.

There is the law of nature. We say, "I am human," and we are. We are limited by the laws governing human beings. These laws demand that man must eat to keep alive and that he must eat certain food to keep healthy. They demand that man must relax at certain periods or suffer emotional or physical break-downs. They demand that he associate with other human beings at certain periods of life—animals or other objects cannot replace these contacts. So men live in cities or in small communities in contact with other human beings. God made us in the be-ginning with these demands in our natures. They are not evil, but good and fine. Solitary confinement of our prisons is one of the worst punishments to mankind.

In one of his parables, Jesus pictures Satan as going into man's freshly planted grain fields. He casts thorn seeds on top of the barley or wheat seeds. The farmer cultivates both kinds of seeds unaware of their mixture. They both spring up about the same time, but, alas, he cannot remove the young weeds without pulling up the young barley or wheat plants, too. This is the way Satan operates in our lives. He does not plant his own half-acre of sin in our lives; he moves in and plants his seeds among the good-seed areas of our lives.

The Good Shepherd does what the sheep can not do for themselves; he removes the poisonous weeds and leads them in to feast on the tender, green, wholesome grass. We cannot trust the laws of nature, for Satan has corrupted them. We need the eyes of the Good Shepherd to grub out the evil from the good, the dangerous from the safe. Human laws of the flesh say, "Let man alone and he will grow up and be alright. Put the right environment around your children and they will grow up to be Christians. They do not need the church, the Bible study, or other activities of the church. Surround them with good friends, send them to the right school, feed them with the right kind of food, dress them correctly and all will be well." Oh, you might not say all that, but we are teaching our children this kind of philosophy by the way we act and by the things we say and do.

Such people would say to their pastor, "Do not preach on sin, or hell, and the evils of our day. Our children do not need that kind of preaching. Tell them about love for one another; about the love of God for them. Teach them to be honest and kind." To such parents, this writer would remind you what happened in the Book of Genesis. Go to your Bibles and read the first three chapters carefully. This will reveal to you Satan's lie to such a "human philosophy." God had surrounded Adam and Eve with a perfect environment. He came down once each day to have communion with them. They had every animal, bird, and fish to do their bidding. They had perfection in nature all around. Not one mark of imperfection could their eyes behold. Of all the trees, plants, and flowers in the Garden, only one was out of bounds for them. And even that tree was beautiful. They had every known fruit to eat that they could have wanted, and yet, in spite of all the perfection around them, these two perfect individuals sinned against their God and brought sin into the human race. Think—really think—if a perfect man or woman, living in a perfect environment, sinned, what chance has an imperfect human being, living in an imperfect society, to live above sin?

God, reminding us of Satan's poisonous weeds, says in His

Word, "All have sinned. All have come short of the glory of God. There is none righteous, no, not one." And God sent Jesus to grub out these poisonous weeds of sin from the human race. As John the Baptist beheld Jesus coming toward him on the banks of the Jordan, he exclaimed under the inspiration of God's Holy Word, "Behold the Lamb of God which taketh away the sin of the world."

Jesus once compared his invitation to men as an invitation to a great banquet. In this parable, he pictures a wealthy man going all-out to give his son the banquet of all banquets. After sending out invitations to carefully selected friends, and getting nothing but refusals, he told his servants to go out into the hedges and the highways and gather all who would come—the poor and the unwanted. When each guest arrived, he was given a special banquet gown. I suppose the lord did not want men in rags and tatters, with the dirt and grime of the streets sitting with his son, so he made special provisions for each to have a new gown. One man came in attired in all his personal finery, but without the banquet gown provided. No doubt, he was one of the select group who had turned down the original invitation, and had suddenly changed his mind. When the Master of the house saw him, and that he did not have on the special gown provided for those at the banquet, he told his servants that this man could not eat at his table—to toss him out into the darkness.

"I am human." Yes, but the human dress is "out of order" in the presence of the Master. It matters not how perfect that dress is, it will not be an acceptable substitute for the dress of the Master. You see, Jesus took out of the human race its seeds of sin—its sinful nature—and left his divine nature in those who came to him for the forgiveness of their sins. A Christian is clothed in the righteousness of Christ. A Christian does live on this earth within sight of his enemies. This is not to be avoided. Sin is the enemy of the soul, but the Christian has nothing to fear from this enemy now. Christ has released man from its chains and bondage. He is free through the blood of the Lamb. Human nature cannot be trusted, but Christ can be trusted. Human nature is limited, but Christ knows no limitation. Human nature might fail, but Christ, never. He meets every need of the human soul, but no need outside of Christ can satisfy the demands of the soul.

A second law controls the actions of the human race—*the law of society.* We do not always do to others what we should do, but we do what we think others expect us to do. Let me illustrate what I mean. Let us say your city has completed a very successful drive for the United Fund. The total pledges and gifts were just short of one million dollars! How was this money raised? Was it given out of love for the needy, the poor, and the less fortunate of our community? If we face up to the truth, we would have to say No. It was raised through the appeal, "This is what society expects of you." If you do not give in the company drive, or as a professional man, you were made to feel, either by your own conscience or by pressure of public opinion, that you had to give or lose face in society—so you gave. If this campaign were pitched on the level of love, your city could not have raised one-tenth that amount.

No nation has ever been saved from an enemy by volunteers only. Oh, yes, many will flock to the flag of their country at the start of any war, but even then, we have to drum up a lot of propaganda. Wars are won by men being drafted, even against their will. However, they do not fight any less bravely than others, once drafted. This is but the law of society. One dare not defy this law or he becomes labeled, and we do not like to become labeled! I am not saying that this is right or wrong; this is not a decision for me to make, because society is a lot older than I. All we can say is that it seems to be the only way society has to protect itself.

Jesus roots out this seed for the Christian. His motivation was on a much higher level. He cared not what the world thought of his position. If Jesus had conformed to the world's accepted idea of the coming Messiah, He would have been received by the Jewish nation with opened arms. If He had complied to man-made laws of theology, He could have been the hero of their day instead of a publicly branded blasphemer. He preached one motive for all that we do—the motive of love. He did not only preach this motive, He lived and died for it. He gave a living and dying demonstration of its application.

A Christian cannot live by the law of society and be a happy Christian. He lives on a higher level. Society says, "Do this or that because this or that is expected of you." Christ says to us, "Do more than is expected of you. If you are asked to go a mile with a Roman soldier and carry his pack—and this was a law—say to him at the end of that mile, say, "Soldier, would you mind if I carried your pack a second mile for you?" Jesus said if you are asked for the shirt off your back by someone who has no shirt, do not stop with the shirt. Give him your coat also. Society says, "One mile you must go or you are an outcast." Christ says, "The first mile is your starting point of giving."

You know, one of the strange things about this philosophy of Christ is that it works! Just try it and see what a difference it will make in your own life, and those around you. It will surprise you how few thorns and poisonous plants you will find in your pasture.

Two barbers were in keen competition with each other in two small shops in a small village. One Saturday, one of these men noticed that his shop was overflowing with customers. After he had finished his last customer, he inquired of him why he had come to his shop for he was not a regular customer. The man replied that the other barber was sick in bed and could not work. Upon hearing this, the barber, after closing his shop, counted his money for the day's work, separating the extra money he had made from the overflow customers, and carried this extra money to his sick competitor saying to him, "I am a Christian and I cannot profit at the expense of another's misfortune." They were no longer competitors, but friends, after this act of love.

Christ, the Good Shepherd, *cleans out the field of religion.* Satan had filled this field so full of his poison that when the Son of God appeared, He had to turn away from the theologians to the laymen of the street. Men were so burdened down with the laws of God imposed upon them by their religious leaders, that they had no time to seek after God himself.

Jesus cleaned the field of theology of all its hidden "do's" and "don'ts" and planted the seed of His grace. "By grace are ye saved. By grace are you kept saved, and by grace you died and by grace ye shall live after death, and by grace ye shall stand before God's throne of judgment." This word "grace" was something new to religion. It had no real spiritual meaning in their language; no words to explain its fullness, so Jesus had to give a demonstration of it. Thus, the trial, the cross, Calvary, the tomb, the resurrection. But the scars on the hands of Jesus had scarcely begun to heal before Satan began to plant his theological poison again in religion. Grace became associated with works, with church membership, and as the years turned into centuries, grace was lost in the forest of religious laws again. Where do we stand today? We need to again go into the valley with Jesus, the Good and only safe Shepherd, look up at the worldly, contaminated, man-made, uprooted laws and philosophies that have been planted in theology as they lay drying out in the presence of the Son of God, awaiting the fires of hell, and then just relax and feast on the abundant green grass of His eternal grace. "For 'tis by grace are ye saved, through faith, not of yourself, not of works, lest ye boast, but the gift of God through His son Christ Jesus." "Thou preparest a table before me in the presence of mine enemies." Let us feast on what He has prepared for us— feast and be contented.

The Future

There's an unknown path before me
    And yet I fear it not;
I know through all the years gone by,
    Whate'er has been my lot,
That a kind and Heavenly Father
    Planned out the way for me;
And I know that in the future,
    Watched over, I shall be.

Yes, I know God's care and kindness
    Will ever with me stay,
To assist me on life's journey,
    And brighten up my way.
So then Welcome! unknown future,
    Bring me whate'er you will—
With God's loving hand to guide me,
    I shall be cared for still!
                    —CORA BAKER HILL

CHAPTER 17

Only Religious Freedom
Can Bring Peace of Mind

"The Lord is my shepherd, I shall not want. He maketh me to lie down in green pastures; He leadeth me beside the still waters; He restoreth my soul. He leadeth me in the paths of righteousness for His name's sake. Yea, though I walk through the valley of the shadow of death, I will fear no evil, for Thou art with me; Thy rod and Thy staff they comfort me. Thou preparest a table before me in the presence of mine enemies." We have gotten down to this last clause in our study of the great Psalm.

We have already noted that each spring of the year in the Far East, a shepherd, before leading his sheep into the pasture, would go ahead of his sheep and grub out the poisonous weeds. He would place these poisonous weeds upon rock pyres built and used by the shepherds of other centuries. When the weeds had dried out by the sun, he would set fire to them. In the meantime, his sheep could graze safely in the pasture. The valley had been prepared for the sheep; with their natural enemy removed, they ate in safety, in the presence of their enemy.

Satan plants his evil seeds in the garden of man. No man, since the first man, Adam, has been able to separate all the good from all the bad. Some men might be able to separate some, but none have been nor shall be able to separate all. God passed a law against sin in the beginning of time. He said that the soul that sinneth shall surely die. This law has not been, or shall it ever be, revoked. Sin brings death—separation. Jesus, the Good

Shepherd, left heaven and God the Father, and came to earth, so that He might roam the fields of man and remove the sin of death, so that man could eat in safety. When man accepts the Good Shepherd into his life, he shares the prepared fields—the life that Christ has prepared for him. He lives in complete spiritual safety all of his earthly life.

We have noted in previous chapters that Satan does not plant his own half-acre of sin in the life of an individual sinner, or in the life of Christians, but he plants his seeds in all areas of our lives. He used the Law of God and made it a stumbling block for man as man tries to feel his way to his God. He took the laws of morals and turned them into booby-traps for man. In this chapter, we want to look at Satan's attempts to replant the field of religion as planted by Jesus before He left for His heavenly home. We need to examine this valley carefully, for death lies among the sheep in every acre of it. Man needs the Good Shepherd to guide him as he eats and lives in this valley. In this chapter, we want to deal with those weeds Satan has planted in religion to rob man, not only of salvation, but also to keep man from having the joy of salvation he is entitled to have. Notice three vital things in religion which Satan tries to corrupt for man.

God planted in man the seed of moral perfection. Freedom of choice is the germinating power of this seed. If man is to be a free agent, he must have the right of choice in moral matters. Man, in the beginning, was made to be a companion to his maker—God. God wanted someone with whom He could share Himself, His goodness, and His love. One cannot force another to love; he cannot require it of another. Love is a response of a free will. God could not force His creatures to love Him, although He could have demanded obedience, generated fear, and made man a servant. Man was made for better things—to become partners with his creator. So God said, "Let us make man in our image. Let us fashion him to fit into our pattern. To live in our orbit." Thus, man was given a freedom no other creature has received—the freedom of free choice—a choice of moral perfection. God enjoyed what He had created, and spent a part of each day with the two people he had created.

Read again the first three chapters of your Bible. Satan, seeing what God had done, steps into the picture with his own seed of destruction. Satan has never had the power to create—make life; but he does have the power to destroy life and ruin life. Because sin originates in the heart of Satan, sin never has the power to create good, but tarnishes all that it touches. Nothing good ever comes from Satan.

So often we hear it said, "Let us pass gambling laws; we can get money for our aged. Let us place a tax on all forms of alcoholic beverages, and get money for our public schools. Let us run gambling houses so that we can get money for our churches and schools." We can secure money for the aged, for our schools and churches by such methods, but have we counted what these methods will cost us in the end? For any plan that is of Satan, harms man and cannot help man. Sin does not lift, but lowers man's moral standards.

If our churches, schools, and fraternal orders breed gamblers over bingo tables and car raffles; if our schools have to be supported by taxes from liquor sales and legalized gambling; and if our aged must be cared for at the expense of our youth's morals, who is the winner in the end? We have played the game with Satan and will reap lost generations of young people. Who is the winner? You know the answer: Satan. You cannot win at the Devil's table. He plays his game with marked cards, and he deals the game himself.

Man's morals and man's free choice of his morals are not to be trusted outside the will of Christ. Man can seek to become the most moral, perfect individual in his community—this is fine, but it is not enough. Moral goodness can be, and is, used by Satan to replace the righteousness of Christ. It becomes a human substitute for the gift of Christ of Calvary.

God does want us to be morally pure in thought and deed, and God wants us to exercise freedom of will in our choices in life. But we need a shepherd to lead us into the right choices of life. God has provided such a shepherd—Christ Jesus, His Son. Man's moral conscience cannot be trusted, for there is no moral perfection outside of the perfection found in God. The Bible says that man "believeth unto righteousness," and "confession is made unto salvation." The perfection that pleases God in the life of an individual is the perfection he sees in the righteousness of His Son, righteousness which should be seen in the life of every believer of Jesus Christ.

Isaiah had a fairly good opinion of himself until he came face to face with God. This experience wrung from his lips the cry, "Woe is me, for I have seen the King. I have seen God, the Holy One. I am a man of impure lips, a man with a sinful heart." Satan would make us believe that our moral goodness is good enough to please God. He takes something which is good and turns it into a thing that separates man from his God. He takes something of divine origin and makes it a tool of hell. He takes something that raises man above the ordinary things of life to cast man into the shadows of despair.

The people among whom Christ lived on earth were great admirers of holy men—the prophets of God. One day Jesus said of the most saintly man of his day, John the Baptist, "He is the greatest prophet of all ages—of men like Isaiah, and others, but he is smaller than the least in the kingdom of God." John, the righteous, the moral, correct man is "less than the weakest Christian." Strange words, indeed. What Jesus was saying is that man's moral goodness, in itself, means nothing in comparison to the gift of God's righteousness, which is made to each one of His children in His kingdom. Jesus was not talking down the goodness of John the Baptist, who died for his righteousness, but He was talking up the inherited righteousness of the Christian, for it is this righteousness of Christ given to the Christian that satisfies God's demands of men. "The Lord is my shepherd, I shall not want . . . Thou preparest a table before me in the presence of mine enemies." It is from Christ, the Good Shepherd, that we receive our food of righteousness and spiritual perfection, and not from man, himself. Satan would have us believe otherwise.

God planted his laws in the religious valleys of man. These laws were not to restrict man's moral selections in life, but to help him make the right selections. The laws of the Bible are not given to man as an end in themselves, but as a means to an end. For example, the first five Commandments (Exod. 20) deal with man's right relationship with God. But man cannot love God because God has commanded it. You cannot command love. God knows this far better than we; God is saying that He wants man to love Him, and that He will respond to man's love toward Him, and that God is worthy of man's love. These Commandments were given to lead us into the love of God, and not merely to be obeyed to make us obedient.

God's commandment regarding adultery is not an end in itself. There is no merit in not committing adultery. God is saying that He made one man for one woman. They were to be joined together by Him and form a divine union. Adultery was an enemy to such a union. This Commandment was to lead society into the ideal life, and, in turn, lead men to know Him in His fullness and glory. Jesus indicated this when He said that for man to think evil or lustful thoughts toward a woman was to commit adultery in his own heart. Man could obey the law of the Old Testament against adultery, but still commit adultery in his heart and mind while standing on the streets of any city in the world. These and other commandments were not given to be "stops signs" to retard the moral traffic on life's highways, but safety signs that make it possible for us to travel safely on the stop street of morals. Through-traffic on stop streets is safe, just as long as someone does not refuse to recognize the stop signs leading onto this highway. Then, not only does the violator get hurt, but often some innocent person does, too.

Satan has taken the laws of God, given by God for the good of man, and as a road map to God himself, and has turned them into detours and an end in themselves. This is what Paul meant when he said that the law was an enemy to man. Satan had taken the law and replaced Christ with them. He says that the thing that was given to man as a means of life had been turned into a thing of death.

Does this mean that the law has become sin? If Satan turns law into a means of salvation, it is sin, for it replaces Christ's sacrifice on the cross. Paul says that the law was the schoolmaster —not in the sense as we understand that word, but in the sense which it was used by Paul. The schoolmaster's job was to see that the child of his master was conducted safely to and from the school each day. He had the responsibility of the safe conduct of the child. He did not teach the child—only carried him to the school where he could be taught.

The laws of God are the schoolmaster for men. They bring us to Christ to be taught by Him; they are guides to God. When we listen to Satan, and look upon these laws as a means of salvation, they become our Gods for us. This is sin.

Here, again, is an example of Satan taking something that is good and doing harm with that thing. Suppose you have a gun to protect your life. A thief finds this gun. He turns the thing against you and would kill you with it. Satan does the same thing with God's holy laws. Man needs a shepherd who can recognize such poisonous weeds, or man would eat them through ignorance, as he eats the grass around them.

The clouds had scarcely closed around the physical form of Jesus as he ascended up to be with the Father, before men were trying to drag men down from this mountain of grace and spiritual freedom to the valleys of rituals to shackle them again with God's holy laws—and this has been going on ever since. Paul cried out to his converts one day saying, "Do not again become entangled. Do not become prisoners to the chains that once bound you, for you were freed from the laws that made you slaves." Christ fulfilled every requirement of every law for every man of all ages. If Satan can make man turn from Christ back again to the law, he has reduced the power of the Cross of Calvary in the lives of the followers of Christ. God's laws are steps that lead to God—to Christ the Saviour. These laws are not God, Himself.

God planted another seed in man's religious valley. This is the seed of His Divine Grace . . . "The Lord is my shepherd, I shall not want . . . Thou preparest a table before me in the presence of mine enemies." Christ roots out the sinful nature in the human race and replaces it with His Divine Grace . . . "By Grace are ye saved, not of works, not of yourself." . . . lest we boast, take credit for what God does, but it is a free gift of God through Christ Jesus . . . This is one of the greatest truths ever revealed to man . . . the gift of God's grace. When God's grace comes into man's life, his nature is changed from the ungodly to the Godly; from the natural to the supernatural; from the mortal to the immortal; from a child of wrath to a child of God. It is changed from the status of an enemy to a favored son; to one out of fellowship with God, to the position of sonship. All this is found in the word "Grace."

Look at what Satan has done to this word "Grace." He has watered it down so cleverly that men have had to add to it— church membership, good works, virtues of Saints of bygone ages, personal sacrifices, and many other things. Man no longer can say, "By Grace are ye saved." He must say, "By Grace, plus church membership, plus this and that." How badly does man need the Good Shepherd to go ahead of him into his fields of religion and theology, to pull out all these poisonous weeds? We again need to learn how to feast upon the simplicity of the Gospel of Christ as given to the Saints of Old. "The Lord is my shepherd." Let Him be that, and He will prepare for us a table in the presence of our enemies.

The Fault Is Mine

Sometimes God seems so far away
   The mists between so dense,
My heart is filled with sudden dread,
   Foreboding, and suspense

The very prayers I utter
   Come straightway back through space—
Too weak to make their faltering way
   Up to the throne of grace.

And then again, God seems so near,
   I cannot but believe;
His faintest whisper rings as clear
   As vesper chimes at eve.

"I never leave thee nor forsake,"
   His gentle whisper saith;
And what had caused my sudden dread
   Was just my lack of faith!

                —Edith M. Lee

CHAPTER 18

What to Do About
the Cuts and Bruises of Life

Some years ago, I visited a model farm. As I was being shown around this farm by the owner, we came to a large pile of pine knots used to start fires during the winter. I asked about them. The farmer replied, "Well, I have enough of them to last this winter and next, but I am worried about the third winter." In those words were written the story of his life. He has been able to acquire much of this world's goods, but he has not learned to enjoy them. He has kept his eyes on the uncertain future—thus, he has lost much of the present.

Future worries have robbed man of much of the joys he should have in this life. The application of the Twenty-Third Psalm to your life will remove such worries. Read this Psalm as you would eat a well-prepared meal. Do not gulp it down as a boy eager to get back to his baseball game. We have been trying to help you do this in these chapters of this book, written on this wonderful scripture. "The Lord is my shepherd, I shall not want. He maketh me to lie down in green pastures; he leadeth me beside the still waters. He restoreth my soul. He leadeth me in the paths of righteousness for His name's sake. Yea, though I walk through the valley of the shadow of death, I will fear no evil, for Thou art with me. Thy rod and Thy staff they comfort me. Thou preparest a table before me in the presence of mine enemies; Thou anointest my head with oil; my cup runneth over."

As we consider that last sentence, "Thou anointest my head

with oil; my cup runneth over," we need to take a short trip to the Holy Land, and visit with the shepherd as he brings his sheep into the sheepfold for the night. He builds this shelter—nothing more than a thorn fence, in many instances, thrown up around his sheep—to protect them from the dangers of the night. The sheep gather at the one opening. The shepherd takes his staff and holds it just high enough for the sheep to pass under it into the sheepfold. As each sheep passes the shepherd, he runs his fingers over their bodies, and scans their bodies with his eyes, looking for cuts, bruises, and other signs of injuries. If he finds something wrong with a sheep, he drops his staff on the body of that sheep, and the sheep will turn aside from the door to await treatment. The shepherd takes him, removes the briers, cleans the cut or bruise, pouring oil into the wound, and then places the nose of the sheep over an earthen jar filled to the brim with fresh water. The sheep plunges his hot nose into the refreshing water. This water jug is never half full, but is running over. The sheep, then refreshed and comforted by the first aid of the shepherd, goes into the sheepfold relaxed for a good night's rest. David was painting this picture for us in the Twenty-Third Psalm, and for men of all ages, thinking not only of sheep, but of God, the Good Shepherd of men. It is a picture of Jesus who called himself the Good Shepherd, who came to give His life for His sheep. We can find three consoling messages in the sentence, "He anointeth my head with oil; my cup runneth over." We will discuss each one in the next three chapters.

The first message we will consider is that this Psalm teaches very clearly that God values the welfare of His sheep. It is so easy for us to forget this great truth. Jesus did not call himself "the Good Shepherd" for lack of a better name for Himself. He used this name with deliberate intent. He was speaking to men who knew the full meaning of such a term. It told them volumes about Himself.

The very appearance of the Son of God, Christ Jesus, upon this earth in the form of man, is an expression of the great love and concern that God had for man, and the supreme expression of this is to be found at Calvary, as this same Son of God takes on the sins of the human race, dying the death of sin for us, thus freeing us from the penalties of sin. Man could no longer say that God does not love the human race, for He proved it at Calvary. It is so easy to ignore this historical fact.

But it is not the purpose of the next three chapters to deal with this glorious fact, but to deal with the position which the Christian has in the sheepfold of God. In this mad, violent world of ours, so often Christians forget what they have in Christ —and, in forgetting, they become victims of worry, trapped by hidden fears and robbed of the joy of salvation and of life. There are entirely too many unhappy Christians in this world. Too many of us have forgotten that God values his sheep. Let us draw a few simple truths from this text and apply them to our lives.

The good shepherd knows that his sheep must feed among the briers, the sharp stones, and the dangers of the fields. His sheep must eat among these dangers if the sheep are to be fed. The shepherd does all that is within his power to protect his sheep from the dangers that might come into the valley to kill his sheep, but he cannot eat for the sheep, nor drink for them, and the grass and water must be out in the world of danger. Every shepherd knows this, and so he makes a daily inspection of each sheep.

God never intended for men to hide themselves away from the world. During one of my vacations, I visited a religious order in a western state. They would not let their members associate with the public or the world in any way. One man was given the responsibility of conducting the tours for visitors, but it was a job looked upon as almost sinful, but one of necessity to gain public support for this particular religious order. These men could not read a newspaper, listen to a radio, or television, visit in the community, and even their mail was closely censored so that no worldly news could creep in. They did not talk to one another except to ask for food and for instructions in religious matters. They said that their world was to be a life of prayer and meditation. Somehow I felt greatly depressed as I left the grounds of that colony. They did not look like happy or contented men. These men had fled from the responsibilities of this life, and were learning to think only of themselves and God. They had committed themselves to a life of solitude. This is not the Bible's idea of devoutness. We are not to flee from this world, which is social suicide, but to live above the world, yet in the world. Jesus took aside the twelve disciples and trained them and sent them out to live with the people, out into the fields of men, where there were briers, sharp stones, and spiritual dangers of every sort. Jesus knew that their spiritual feet would be bruised; they would pick up thorns in their feet, and have their noses infected with the diseases of their day, but he also knew that when they returned each evening, He would remove the briers, pour oil in their cuts, and destroy the disease. And the world now was a better place in which to live because of their efforts, and God's kingdom was enlarged.

A Christian is not to live alone; he is not to withhold himself from the world. The lost sheep of God are not to be found within the church walls, but on the sidewalks of the world. The Christian has to earn a living often standing beside a man who is profane; who is sinful both in thought and language. The Christian schoolboy has to sit beside a boy who cheats, lies, and steals. The businessman has to compete for success with a man who ignores the Christian rules of conduct, honesty, and fairness. So often I hear someone say, "I cannot be a Christian and stay in business," or "A Christian cannot run this kind of business and succeed." We forget that God's plan for man is for him to live in the world, but not to forget that God knows our every danger, temptation, and risk that we take, and to know Him as our Comforter and Companion. Sheep must feed among dangers, but they feed under the watchful eye of the shepherd who loves them. So does the Christian.

A second truth to be gleaned from this scripture is that the shepherd knows that the greatest danger to a sheep is not in his exposure to danger, but in the untreated wound suffered through such exposure, in the unremoved brier or thorn, and the untreated cut. It is impossible for us to live in this world day after day and not pick up a few of its thorns and briers or receive a few cuts and bruises. Our greatest danger will not be in these things themselves, but in our failure to have a daily examination by our Shepherd and to have his daily treatment of them. A thorn becomes only a small annoyance if removed at once, but if left in the body for long, it can cause the loss of a limb, and even can result in death. A small cut is of little harm if given prompt attention, but if left uncleaned and exposed, it can turn the whole body into a thing of pain and can also result in death.

Sheep, in their dumb and silent way, have learned that they need the shepherd's hand to find the thorns, briers, cuts, and bruises in their bodies. They have learned that pain is quickly removed if they are obedient to the care of their shepherd. Sheep have learned this truth, but so few of us have. We hear a cutting, critical remark about ourselves, and hold this in our hearts for days, and even years, brooding upon it until it has poisoned our entire life. We have a failure and we live with this failure until it eats away all of our confidence. We are tempted, and we yield. We are ashamed of this weakness, but we cover it up. We think we can hide it from God, our Master. It goes unconfessed, unattended, and it grows and grows until we are spiritually sick all over.

The greatest sin is not in the act of sinning, but in remaining in sin after we have fallen. To sin is bad, but to live in sin is worse. Two men were talking about the death of a mutual friend. One asked, "What caused his death?" The other said, "He fell into the river," but before he could finish his explanation, the other man cut into his conversation and concluded for him, "He drowned because he fell into the river." The other man replied, "No, he did not drown because he fell into the river, but because he remained in the river after he fell." Herein is our greatest danger—the unremoved thorn and the unattended cut. All of us will get our share of these as we live and work and move through our world. The Good Shepherd will protect us the best He can, but He cannot nor will He make every selection for us in life. We have to make our own decisions. We are creatures of habit, and other people's habits wear off on us if we are not on the alert every second. Our greatest danger is not in the mistakes we make, but in not recognizing their presence in our lives and in not removing them at once. We need to be aware of this great danger.

This leads us to a final thought in this chapter. We said that a good shepherd valued his sheep. This fact is demonstrated by this sentence, "Thou anointest my head with oil; my cup runneth over." Thus, he stands each day, as the shades of night begin to close in on him and his sheep, inspecting each individual sheep for cuts, bruises, and briers before turning the sheep in for their night's rest. He cannot wait until morning for such inspection, for in the morning that cut will be infected, and that thorn will become a dangerous sore which might be beyond his limited medical resources to heal, and another sheep might be lost. Here is the important thought. Each cut, bruise, or brier needs daily personal attention from the shepherd.

One day, the disciples asked Jesus to teach them how to pray. There is one thought in this model prayer that is closely associated with the thoughts we have been considering in this chapter. Jesus said that we are to ask, "Give us this day our daily bread." He meant more than just a request for a loaf of bread for that particular day. The people to whom Jesus spoke baked their bread days in advance, so why pray for bread when your kitchen contained a week's supply? This was more than a request for a loaf of bread. It was a request for God to give the body the care it needed for each day. It was a request for wisdom to select the right kind of foods needed for the body to make it strong and useful. It was a request for the right things for the body and the wisdom to keep out that which might harm the body. This is a daily need of man.

As we come to the end of each day, each child of God needs to pass in review before the Good Shepherd and let His spiritual fingers go over our bodies to discover anything that should not be there—to find it and remove it for us. We need to kneel or stand quietly before Him and let His eyes examine our minds and hearts to see if the world has not planted something within us that will harm us.

Millions of sleeping pills are sold each year in America. Do you know why? Because we are trying to go to bed with the briers and thorns of the world lodged in our spiritual skins. Sheep rest well because the things they have picked up in the world each day have been found by the Good Shepherd and have been removed by him. He has poured his healing oil into their wounds and they have been refreshed by his cool water. Thus, they enter into the sheepfold clean and relaxed.

When was the last time you prayed to God before going to bed at night? Or the last time you read His Word, and sought His cleansing forgiveness? Prayer will give you a better night's sleep than pills—try it. If a sheep needs daily inspection by his shepherd, how much more do we need this, for our world is filled with more thorns and sharp stones than any pasture in Palestine.

A snake can be captured by a spider. The spider catches a snake sleeping and begins to touch his body with a thin web— so light that he cannot feel it. This is done hundreds and hundreds of times. If the snake should be aroused before the spider is finished, he seems to think nothing of the silken threads on his body and does not rub them off. Later, when he does try to move, he finds himself incased in thousands of filmy, silken threads that hold him helpless until death overtakes him.

Man is not destroyed by one great sin, one great fall; but he is destroyed by those unremoved small things in his life that become big with time. We need a daily visit from our Shepherd to keep us free from the small infections of life.

Our Lives

> Can you say today in parting
> With the day that's slipping fast,
> That you've helped a single person
> Of the many you have passed.
>
> Did you waste the day, or lose it,
> Was it well or poorly spent?
> Did you leave a trail of kindness
> Or a scar of discontent?
>
> As you close your eyes in slumber,
> Do you think God would say
> You have made the world much better
> For the life you lived today?

CHAPTER 19

You Cannot Remove Certain Thorns from Your Life

In our last chapter, we studied the verse in the Twenty-Third Psalm, "Thou anointest my head with oil; my cup runneth over," as it reveals the shepherd's value of his sheep. David was speaking as an experienced shepherd. He had spent most of his younger years with sheep. He had brought his sheep into the sheepfold thousands of times. He had examined each of his sheep hundreds of times, as it approached the entrance to the sheepfold each night, and searched its body for embedded thorns, briers, and cuts. He had bathed many cuts and scratches, and removed many briers from sensitive noses. He had carried unnumbered jugs of water with which to refresh feverish sheep.

In the last chapter, we pointed out that a shepherd would stand at the entrance to his sheepfold, the pen in which he placed his sheep each night for protection. He would lay his staff across this entrance just high enough for the sheep to pass under it. He would then examine each sheep carefully for cuts and bruises. If he found any, he would remove all the foreign matter, bathe the wound, and then pour olive oil into it. He would then refresh each sheep with a cool drink of water from a large water jug he always kept near the entrance. A shepherd does this because he values his sheep. A good shepherd will take care of his sheep daily. God does the same for all of us, His sheep, and David gives great emphasis to this wonderful truth in this Psalm.

There is a second truth in this line, "Thou anointest my head

with oil; my cup runneth over." Not only does it teach us that
a shepherd values and cares for his sheep, but the sheep have
learned to value the daily care of their shepherd. They accept
his care without protest, and with evidences of appreciation. Let
us examine three simple truths growing out of this thought.

The shepherd is the inspector, not other sheep, nor the sheep
itself. 'Tis the shepherd who stands at the entrance to inspect
his sheep. He determines their fitness, their needs, and their
treatment. Sheep cannot do this for themselves because they are
not equipped, either by nature or by training, to do so. If one
sheep tried to remove a thorn from another, he would only force
it deeper into the body of the other. Though it's unlikely, a
sheep might be able to remove some thorns from some parts of
its body; but he could do nothing about thorns in other areas
of his body. He needs a shepherd.

The truth here for us is so obvious that we are apt to ignore
it. And yet, so few of us practice it. Have you ever heard one
Christian criticize another? Each of us has his own standard
of values, and woe to that one who does not measure up to it.
Man is not to stand in moral judgment of another. Man stands
and falls before his own Master. Christians are more guilty, to
a greater degree, in this matter than non-Christians. This is one
of our greatest weaknesses. Jesus faced this problem in his age.
Do you remember what he said one day to a group of church-
men? "You try to remove a tiny splinter, a speck of dust, from
your brother's eye, and overlook the plank in your own eye."
Paul warns the early Christians that they were not to stand in
judgment of each other, saying that each servant shall stand in
judgment before his own master, and not before other servants
or other masters.

Sheep cannot remove thorns or briers from their own bodies.
They need the kind hands of a shepherd. Neither can man remove the briers and thorns he gets from this world. He needs
help. "Thou anointest my head with oil." Thou, God, anointest

my head! I recall in my early years in the seminary a great hurt was done to me by my best friend. He was wrong in his action, and this added to my hurt. I found myself beginning to hate his very presence and to resent the sound of his name. I knew that this was hurting my own spiritual life, and I tried to forget it all, but without success. I determined that each day I would retire alone into the prayer room of our Seminary and pray for this man until my own heart had lost its hurt. It was not easy at first. Oh, it was easy to say words and call it prayer. It was easy to tell God how hurt I was over this man's actions, and to turn him over to the care of God, but wishing deep down in my heart that God would give him a good thrashing. This kind of prayer did me no good. Then I found myself praying for my own self, asking God to give me the forgiving spirit and then, and only then, was the victory won. God did remove from my life the thorn this man had placed there. I could not have done this myself, for I had tried and had failed.

If you hold anything against another, regardless of who is to blame, you cannot remove this thorn yourself. If you allow it to linger on in your life, it will be because you have not turned it over to the Good Shepherd to have it removed. He never fails to remove the thorn, and then pours healing oil into the wound. The honest truth about most of these hurt feelings among Christians is that we get a certain amount of joy out of suffering. It makes us feel like a martyr, and this, in turn, makes us feel morally better than others. The Bible says that a Christian is not to let the sun go down on his anger, on his resentment toward another Christian. The Bible also teaches that when we approach a worship service and remember ill that another has against us—and Jesus is implying here that this ill has caused us to sin in our own hearts—for us to leave our gift on the altar, seek out this brother, and get our heart right toward him, and then come back and worship with clean hands and a calm heart. Sheep seem to be smarter than a lot of professed Christians. They do not like to bed down for the night with briers, thorns, or cuts unattended by their shepherd.

I wonder what would happen to the churches of America if all the members of our churches would act like sheep and turn daily to the Master to have Him remove the thorns from their lives—if each of us would stop tying to run the lives of others, and if each of us who has received a hurt from another, or who has hurt another, would go to that one and seek his or her forgiveness. What would happen? I think I can tell you. We would have a great revival of love break out in our churches and, in turn, this would have such a profound effect upon our nation. We could not accommodate the people who would flock to our churches. We would have a living preview of heaven on earth. Yes, this Psalm teaches that the shepherd, and not the sheep, is the inspector, the daily inspector of the sheep.

The second truth from this subject, "Thou anointest my head with oil; my cup runneth over," is that the sheep seem to welcome the relief that comes from the hands of their shepherd. If sheep could talk, I imagine they would say something like this: "Yes, I do stand complacently before my shepherd as his tender hands run over my body. I do not cry out when he has to probe for a deeply embedded thorn, or go into an open wound to remove particles of stone or glass. It does hurt very much, but I have learned that in hurting me this way, the shepherd is protecting me from a greater hurt later on. After all, I cannot blame him for my pain. He did not put the thorn in my body, or make the cut in my side. I got these out in the pasture filling my stomach with grass. He has done what he could to protect me from these things, and I cannot blame him."

We are so quick to flare back at God when we have some disappointment, some hurt, some failure, some loss or sickness. When God has to step in to remove some of the things we have put into our lives that are harmful to us, we resent the pain. God never makes a mistake. God never does wrong. God never hurts any of his children to be hurting them, but He has to perform many a spiritual operation on us to remove things that would cripple us or even kill us spiritually if left to remain.

All of us are familiar with the story of Job. He was accused by Satan before God as using God for a good thing, and this was the charge that Satan made to God when he said, "Job is serving you because you are good to him. Take away your blessings from his life and he will curse you to your face." God said, "Alright, he is in your hands. All he has is yours except his life." Job lost his children, his wealth, and his health. His so-called friends said to him one day, "What is the use of struggling? God has forsaken you." And his wife added her voice to this lament by saying, "Curse your God and die. At least you will get out of your misery." Job's reply has lived through the ages. He said, "Though He slay me, I will not blame my God, nor will I defame His name. Let Him do to me what He will, but He shall still be my God." Job trusted God, his Good Shepherd, even when living in the greatest distress.

Many times God has to hurt us in order to save our lives. As one of our great painters of history was finishing a mural in one of the churches of Europe many years ago, he was working on a scaffold high above the floor. He suddenly began to back off from one of his figures to study its coloring. He forgot his danger and was on the very edge of the scaffold when one of his helpers looked up from his work and saw the master's danger. He knew that if he yelled, it would cause him to turn and fall, so he threw a paint brush into the nearly completed painting. The artist sprang forward to save his work and cried out, "You fool, you have ruined it." The young helper said, "Yes, I did, but I have saved your life. You can paint another figure into the picture, but you could not have regained your life."

God often has to step in and ruin pictures in our lives in order that He might save our lives, so that we can paint better pictures later. He has to hurt us to keep our hurts from destroying us. Sheep have learned this from their shepherds. We need to learn this about our Shepherd.

Sheep have learned a third thing about this daily inspection. The relief they get from the hands of their shepherd offsets the temporary pain they must undergo to have their wounds treated. Good sheep know this and they are always obedient to the will of their shepherd. Thus sheep do not shrink from these daily inspections. Again we are forced to conclude that in some matters sheep are smarter than Christians. Sheep will seek out the master's care and accept it when they are hurt, but too many of us will forsake the Good Shepherd under similar circumstances.

I have observed through my years as a minister and pastor, that people rarely come to me when they are hurt with me. I generally find it out from others, or by their absence from the church. Is this true of your life? So many times if those people had come to me at once, there would have been no damage done to them or to me. People become offended over such strange things. Once a woman carried ill feelings toward me for several months just because I did not give her hand a vigorous enough handshake as she passed out the door of the church one Sunday. When she finally came to me months later, she said she knew that I was angry with her that day over something, because of the type of handshake I had given her that morning. You say, "Silly woman! What an imagination!" and I will have to agree with you, but look into your life and you might be surprised how many friendships you have lost for reasons just as silly. The Bible says that if we are offended, we are to go to the one who has given us offense and make it right with that one.

Rarely do people who are sick call their minister. He has to find it out by checking the hospital records when he visits the hospital. And yet, how many of us have not been guilty of saying, "I was sick and no one came to see me; no, not even the pastor of my church." This starts a chain reaction against all churches and all ministers. We either do not know or forget that it is the responsibility of the one who is sick to notify their minister. The sheep come to their shepherd for his inspection. The Bible says when we are sick, we should call the elders of the church. I sometimes wonder if people are not deliberate in these things so that they might have an excuse to justify their own neglect of others and their responsibilities to their church. You rarely hear of someone who visited the sick complaining that they are not visited when they are sick.

Sheep do not make this mistake. They go to the shepherd at once; they stand daily inspection for their bruises and cuts. They have learned that it is more pleasant to have such things removed each day than to suffer through the night with the pain of an unremoved thorn, or an untreated cut. Healthy sheep do not enjoy pain; neither does a healthy Christian. If you are carrying a grudge or holding a hurt toward another, you are not a healthy Christian. You need to go to the Good Shepherd for an inspection.

A Christian ought to carry a hurt or ill toward another only as long as it takes to get to the one who has caused it and make it right. Daily inspection by the shepherd will help us to find the small briers, the small cuts that can and will develop into more serious sores later.

That Christian who never attends church, who never gives and who is critical of his church, is nursing many cuts, bruises, thorns, and briers picked up in his world. He has refused to turn to the Good Shepherd who would remove them from his or her life. He does not enjoy the relief he would get by the Master's removal of them. He shrinks from the temporary pain he might suffer in having them removed. He has not learned what all sheep know—the comfort that comes after they are removed. He cannot say, "Thou anointest my head with oil; my cup runneth over."

You Can't Fool God

You can fool the hapless public,
You can be a subtle fraud,
You can hide your little meanness
    But you can't fool God!

You can advertise your virtues,
You can self achievement laud,
You can load yourself with riches,
    But you can't fool God!

You can criticize the Bible
You can be a selfish clod,
You can lie, swear, drink, and gamble,
    But you can't fool God!

You can magnify your talent,
You can hear the world applaud.
You can boast yourself somebody,
    But you can't fool God!

CHAPTER 20

It Is No Sin to Be Happy

Some people live and act as if it were a sin to be happy. I have known good church people who were afraid to smile—at least, they gave everyone that impression. Some people believe that life on this earth is more to be endured than enjoyed. Such people either have not read the Twenty-Third Psalm, or do not understand it. Neither have they walked through the four Gospels in our Bible with Jesus. He was a scatterer of sunshine and happiness wherever He went. God wants His children to be happy.

Happiness is a sign of good health. Good health is not limited only to the physical body. The well-balanced personality must have a healthy mind and spirit also. The kind of theology we believe has much to do with our mental and spiritual health.

I was playing golf with a minister one day and we were discussing the joys we got out of life. It was pointed out that whenever a group of preachers of a certain church got together, there was much laughter, and the warmth of fellowship was visible. It was also pointed out that some other ministers we knew, from another denomination, never seemed to be happy, and lived a life of great dignity, discipline and stiffness. They seemed to have lost the music from their lives. I suggested that their theology might be the difference. One could not be happy within without a positive assurance of his own salvation and a sense of close relationship with God. A child cannot get much pleasure out of his toys when he knows that his parents might not be approving of his conduct, and that he can never be sure that he is pleasing them. Neither can man, be he preacher, priest, rabbi, or men in the pew.

God wants all men to be happy. David, the author of the Psalm we have been considering in this book, is giving us the secret to a happy life. Happiness for man is founded upon the same relationships sheep have with their shepherd and the shepherd has with his sheep. Happiness and good health for sheep rests upon what the shepherd does for his sheep, and upon the reactions or response of the sheep to the shepherd's care. The same is true of men in their relationship with God. Now, consider this verse from the Twenty-Third Psalm for the proof of this thought: "Surely goodness and mercy shall follow me all the days of my life." This suggests three thoughts for human happiness—and remember God wants all of us to be happy in this life.

First, it gives the assurance that it is a false theology that would have us believe that one must be unhappy here on this earth if we are to be happy after death. The word for "man" in the Bible is a word that describes the position man has before his God. The word "Anthrophos" means the animal who walks with his face upward toward his God. God made all other animals to walk with their faces downward. Man gets his joy and happiness from the direction in which his face is pointed—from up above. Man can never be happy if he lives with his face downward— away from God.

When we were children, we were often surprised how quickly mother would detect when we had done some wrong act. We thought mother had some unusual power that helped her see in the dark or behind closed doors. What we did not know was that after we had done something we should not have done, we were afraid to look mother in the eye. The downward cast of our eyes told her that we had been disobedient in something.

While I was pastor of a church in Mobile, Alabama, one of the gateways into Florida, a lot of drifters from the north on their way to Florida called on me during the early fall of each year.

Their hard luck stories were always the same, with few variations. These men and women would not look right into my eyes as they related their tales of woe. They knew they were not telling the truth. The man out of fellowship with his God reacts the same toward his God. He does not walk with his face turned in the direction of God, but walks with his eyes elsewhere. The animal gets his joy from the ground, from the grass and herbs, thus he walks with his eyes downcast toward his source of joy. The longer man is separated from his God and seeks his happiness apart from his God, the more he becomes in his thinking and actions like the lower forms of creation.

God made man to be happy—to walk with his face upward toward the source of his happiness—God. Nothing pleases God more than to hear the joyful laughter of his children—to know that they are healthy and happy.

I had a wonderful father. He lived in an age of great moral and social changes, and he was a great thinker, ahead of his time. He had to pay the price for crusading for the things he believed were best for his country. Attempts were made to ruin his character, and even his life, by the forces of the underworld. Dad never revealed any fear or anxiety to his children, or to mother. He lived with a smile on his face and a song in his heart. He smiled so much that when he died his face had the natural wrinkles of a smile; a smile grew into his face. I knew no other man who got such a great kick out of life, or more joy than he from life. Children loved him and dogs followed him on the streets. Psychologists tell us children and dogs are the best judges of character. And when he died, his city mourned his passing. If there were no heaven to receive him, the joy he got from living justified his life.

God wants man to be happy, but man cannot be happy with his face turned away from his God. And one does not have to be unhappy on this earth to be assured of happiness after death. I often hear some young married couple say, "I know it is a sin to be so happy, but I can't help it." Nonsense. Your happiness makes your God happy, too.

"Surely goodness and mercy shall follow me all the days of my life." This ought to be so, and will be so, if we are God's children, through Christ. For God made this world so that He could make man happy. When you get "down in the emotional dumps" of life, lose your joy of living, get so pressed down with problems of life, take time out to look around this world that is your world. It is a beautiful creation!

During the battle for Sicily, I often swept the horrors of dying friends from my mind by watching God paint a beautiful sunset, using the sky and Mediterranean Sea as his canvas. Later, in Europe, when loneliness seemed to be crushing out all hope of seeing my family again, I would look up into the purple Bavarian mountains, into God's revealed beauty, and again gain new strength. Who can awaken to the song of a mockingbird in the middle of the night and not feel some of the beauty of God in the song of a happy bird singing in God's radiant moonlight? God has made this world so that He could make man happy, for He wants man to be happy.

What minister has not stood at the foot of an open grave, seeing the grief on the faces of children, or of a heartbroken husband or wife, and not ask himself the question, "Will this wound ever heal?" But God has a way of healing these wounds, using the salve of His Divine Grace. Those tear-stained faces will again be creased with smiles. New lives will take root in the valley of tears to enrich that life even to a greater degree by the sufferings of the soul. God has made it possible for the lonely husband or wife to rebuild the broken pieces of life into one of great joy and happiness.

A classmate once told me how he tried to console a mutual preacher friend who had just lost his wife. As he lay stricken in grief, the friend said to him something like this: "Do not have such hopeless grief, for you know that your wife was a devout

Christian and she is safe in the arms of her Saviour. You are young and in time even this great wound will heal. God might even lead you to another wonderful companion to share your work and your future." Before this good friend could finish what he was trying to say, the grieving minister sprung to his feet and said in anger, "Don't talk like that. I feel like striking you with my fist for even suggesting that I would ever marry again." A year later, this man was happily married to a lovely Christian woman who is making him a splendid wife. The grieving minister was sincere in what he said to my friend, but he had forgotten that God has made this world so that He might make us happy, even when we have to pass through the valleys of the shadow of death. Happy children are healthy children and God wants us to be healthy and happy. "Surely goodness and mercy shall follow me all the days of my life."

I do not share in the theology of some who would have men rush through this life as fast as we can, living and thinking of the glories of heaven, and ignoring the beauties of this world, for my Bible tells me that God made man to live in, and to enjoy the beauties of this world. If one can do this, he is better prepared to enjoy the greater beauties of the next world. This world is only a proving ground for us, a place of preparation, so that we might get the most from the glories that are to come to all the children of God in the life beyond the grave.

There is another great truth to be found in this text, "Surely goodness and mercy shall follow me all the days of my life," and that is: God gives to each man just as much of His Goodness and Mercy as man can receive without injury to the personality of man. God never makes the mistake as so many parents do of giving their children too much of something, thus, ruining their values of life.

Have you ever wondered why there are so many poor Christians in this world? The answer can be found in this text. For example, in the Bible, God says to us that if we give back to him one-tenth of all that He gives us, that He will bless us in a material way, plus in other ways. Now, if a wealthy person, or corporation would say to you, "I will make you wealthy if you will use that which I give to you, according to my directions. These directions I shall make are to protect you from being destroyed by that which I give you. One of my requirements is that you give back to me one dime out of every dollar I give you." Would you accept this offer? I think that we all would! Now, God has said the same thing to every Christian, but few of us will accept this offer from God. We will not believe it. We are like the man in a Chinese parable. He was a beggar. Another man had mercy on him and gave him nine of the ten coins he had on his person. The beggar followed him down the street, thanking him for his gift, and in the crush of the crowd, he was able to steal the tenth coin also.

God gives to each of us only the things with which he can trust us—or the amount that does not permit us to destroy ourselves or our spirituality. Even then, God often has to stand by and watch us abuse Him, even with the minimum of His giving.

Man's standard of success rarely is God's measurement of success. Man thinks he can find happiness and success in the acquiring of great wealth, prestige with his fellow man, or in exercising authority over others. God measures our success by the way we use our abilities for Him, others, and ourselves. Look around you. The people who seem to get the most from life and seem to be the happiest are not always those who have the biggest bank accounts, drive the biggest cars, or wear the best clothes.

One of the many lessons I learned during my overseas duty in the last war was that a man could be happy with very, very little. Life is reduced to very simple terms in combat. A letter from home, a cup of hot coffee, the relief you feel to hear the voices of your buddies after a bomb or shell has exploded near you, seeing the sun rise again, and knowing that you are alive for another day. A dry foxhole on a cold night is life itself. Such small things had little meaning for us before combat service.

Happy is the man or woman who has learned to accept the daily goodness and mercy of God each day—accept them with the keen knowledge that such things are from a God who loves them. Happy is that person who accepts these gifts and enjoys them to the fullest, for God has given them to us to make us happy.

If you feel that life has cheated you, take down the ledgers of your life and study them; take an inventory of your life. You will find that you have abused and misused much of what God has given you. You have refused to accept God's way—God's will in the usage of the things he gave you. Sheep know that happiness for them is to live within their sheepfold and to stay with the flock no matter where their shepherd leads them. Many of us have yet to learn this important lesson.

I knew of a mother who asked her pastor to plead to God for the life of her son. He cautioned her about making such a demand and suggested that they ask for his life if it were God's will to spare him. She said she was not concerned about God's will, in this matter, if it meant the loss of her child. God did spare the boy, but this mother lived to see him tried for murder, and to die in the electric chair. As her son was being executed, she cried, "I would rather that my son had died when he was a child than die like this—the murderer of another." She had that choice once—not the choice of life or death for her child, but the choice of trusting the will of God. God knows all; this we know from the study of His word, the Bible, and when we put alongside of this fact another great fact—God wants us to be happy in this life, and will give us only those things that will make us happy if we are willing to accept them—then we cannot blame God for our lack of happiness on this earth. We have learned the secret of happiness when we learn to accept God's will for our lives. "Surely goodness and mercy shall follow me all the days of my life" . . . and they will follow every child of God.

His goodness and mercy are for us to enjoy daily. Are you sharing in them?

O, Christ, the Way

O Christ, the Way, the Truth, the Life,
Show me the living way,
That in the tumult and the strife
I may not go astray.

Teach me Thy Truth, O Christ, my Light,
The Truth that makes me free,
That in the darkness and the night
My trust shall be in Thee.

The Life that Thou alone canst give,
Impart in love to me,
That I may in Thy presence live,
And ever be like Thee.

—GEORGE L. SQUIER

CHAPTER 21

God's Daily Care of You Brings Its Own Rewards

"Thou anointest my head with oil; my cup runneth over." Healthy sheep are the results of the shepherd's daily care.

Dr. Eugene Antrim, a minister in Oklahoma City, tells of an experience he had a few years ago. He was standing by a hotel window which faced a city street, when he heard the squeal of streetcar brakes, then the cry of an injured man. As he watched, he saw a large crowd gather around the streetcar which had stopped in front of the hotel.

Dr. Antrim hurried out to see what had happened. He saw a man under the streetcar suffering terribly. Efforts to get the man out from under the streetcar were unsuccessful. The police car came, and workmen from the streetcar line, but they soon saw that it would be necessary to send for some heavy equipment from the carbarn to extricate the injured man, and that would take some time. The man was crying hysterically, "Get me out, get me out of here! Please!"

It was apparent that the shock of the accident, the pain, and the fear had made the man hysterical. What was to be done with him during the half hour or more it would take to get the machinery on the spot to lift that streetcar and release him? A simple, ordinary man, a badly dressed bystander, solved that problem. He came out of the crowd, crawled under the car, lay down beside the victim, put his arms around him and began to talk kindly and softly into his ears. The man calmed down, stopped his frantic crying, his hysteria left, his fears were calmed, and he smiled into the stranger's face lying beside him and said, "Thank you, friend."

In a half hour, the lifting equipment came from the carbarn and lifted the streetcar that pinned the man down. The ambulance took him away, and the man who lay down beside him quietly disappeared into the crowd, never to be found again.

A very successful pastor among laboring people was asked his key of success. The reply was given by one of his members, "He walks where we walk." . . . "Thou anointest my head with oil; my cup runneth over." God takes care of His sheep, and to do this, He must be near His sheep at all times. You never see flocks of sheep on the open range without a shepherd near them. Healthy sheep are the results of the shepherd's daily care. The presence of our Good Shepherd calms our fears, quiets our nerves, and fills our hearts with contentment. Nature does the rest for us, and the results are healthy children of God.

A few years ago, a few wild ducks and a couple of wild geese came in to rest one day on the small lake on the golf course of the Mobile Country Club. They were tired and hungry and every line of their bodies spoke of fatigue. They found food here, and one of the ground keepers began to feed them each day. These fowl were still on the lake the last time I played golf there. They had lost their fear of the golfers; they were things of beauty, well fed, contented, and healthy. They were once wild ducks and geese, fearful of all things around them, hungry most of the time, and with only a short lifespan ahead of them. They had lived in fear, for in every marsh or lake they flew into for food or shelter, might be found a hunter. Now, in the beauty and quietness of this small lake on the golf course were no guns or enemies. Only peace, plenty and promise. When other ducks flew over and called to them, they did not respond—they were now "cared-for" ducks. Theirs was the better life. This is the point I wish to make: "cared-for" sheep are better sheep than wild sheep—sheep without a shepherd. "Cared-for" sheep are not as nervous as wild sheep. They live longer, and get more from the years they do live than wild sheep. They give more to their shepherd. "The Lord is my shepherd, I shall not want . . . Thou anointest my head with oil; my cup runneth over." A wild sheep has no shepherd and lives most of his life in want. He has no shepherd to anoint his head with oil, to soothe his cuts and bruises, and he has no one to pull out the thorns and briers from his body. There is a vast difference between uncared for sheep and those cared for by the shepherd. Put one of each together, and even the untrained eye can see this difference.

A friend of mine, some years ago, bought a pure-blooded Tennessee walking horse for his wife. It was a beautiful animal. As my friend was pointing out to me the good points of this prized animal, he began to slap, with his hands, sensitive points on the body of the horse. The horse did not move, nor show any signs of fear or nervousness. My friend then explained that these horses had been bred so carefully over the years that natural fears and sensitiveness toward man had been bred out of them. They had been reared with such close supervision from man, they held no fear of man. No wonder it was such a desirable animal. Every line of its body portrayed good breeding and care. He was a "cared-for" horse.

So often we hear someone say, "I am not a Christian, but I am just as good as any Christian I know." This is not so, nor can it be so. Being a Christian is more than being good in actions or conduct. In fact, moral actions have nothing to do with the question. All men ought to be morally good for their own sakes, their families' sake, and for the good of society, whether they are Christians or not. Christ did not come to change the moral clothes of man; He came to give him a new nature so that He, Christ, could restore man again into the sheepfold of God. Man, through his sins, had left the sheepfold of God and was wandering in the spiritual wilderness without a shepherd. Jesus came to "seek and to save that which was lost."

Too long has religion majored on fear. The appeal is made too often on the plane of God's punishment for sin, and we do not spend enough time in explaining to men what God is offering man. Hell does await every lost man. Sin does separate man from God and this separation is an eternal one in hell. There is no second chance taught in the Bible for those who go out of this world without sharing in the forgiveness of God as found in and through Christ Jesus, His Son. All this is true, but there is more to God than His willingness to save man from an eternal hell after death.

Salvation *is* salvation from hell, but what is more wonderful than this is the willingness of God to share Himself with man—not just in eternity, but here on earth. When one becomes a Christian, God, through His Holy Spirit, abides with man. It is this abiding Spirit of God that will "anoint our head with oil" and keeps our cups running over. This is more than a figure of speech—it is a reality in the life of every Christian. When we give our hearts, souls, and lives to the Good Shepherd, through faith in His Son, God assumes complete ownership of our lives forever. If there is one truth which has endured through the ages, it is this one—God cares for His own. God does not forsake one single sheep. "The Lord is my shepherd; I shall not want" is a fact as real to the Christian as life itself. You cannot be a Christian without Christ being real to you.

Salvation from an eternal hell is wonderful, but the peace that comes with the presence of God's Holy Spirit to every Christian, is even more wonderful! It is this presence that makes "cared-for" sheep better than wild sheep.

"Thou anointest my head with oil; my cup runneth over." Picture the sheep as they come into the sheepfold for the night. As each pauses at the sheep door for his daily inspection by his shepherd, he wonders if those soft, gentle hands will find the hidden thorn in his side, and if he can detect the fever in his body? He does not have to worry very long, for the skilled hands of the shepherd quickly find and remove, not just that one thorn but every brier, and pours oil into every scratch. These sheep go into the sheepfold and get a good night's rest, and out into the chosen pastures of tomorrow. As a result of this care, these sheep will produce more and better wool than wild sheep. This is the second fact about "cared-for" sheep. They are more productive for their owners.

The life function of sheep is to produce wool and/or food. Good wool producers rarely, if ever, become table providers. Sheep that have a shepherd can, and do, outproduce wild sheep in wool, not only in quantity, but also in quality. Wild sheep are hunted, not for their wool, but for their meat and for sport. But wild sheep are not all in the mountains.

There are entirely too many wild sheep within our churches. They are poor producers for the Kingdom of God. A sheep that does not care about his church, never attends its worship services, or attends now and then, becomes a neglected sheep, and little, if any, wool is harvested by God from that life. It has been said that 15 percent of church members carry 95 percent of the entire load of the church. They do the teaching, visiting of the sick, and the giving. None of us would think that the movie houses of America ought to give us a free ticket to all their shows, or that all colleges should give us free tickets to all their football games, or that the grocer, the milkman, or the clothier ought to consider it a privilege to keep us fed or clothed. Yet 85 percent of our church members look to God and their church for all their spiritual food, with never a thought of their own responsibility toward God or His church. They want a church building—not just an ordinary building, either, but the best, air-conditioned, modern, and beautiful—but leave the responsibility to others to maintain it for them. I know of a church member, a man who has a good job in the city, who is faithful to at least one service each week, and would be considered "active." Yet, his pledge card indicates twenty-five cents per week to the support of his

church—not even the price he would pay for a package of cigarettes. It would not pay for the materials his church furnishes
him—the heat, or the air-conditioned building, or his part for mis-
sions, or the other benefits he receives from his church. Not
much wool for God from this sheep. But the greater loser is not
God, but this man, himself. There are thousands just like him
in our churches across America. Perhaps you might be one!
God's care of such a person is wasted as far as any profit to God
or to His Kingdom is concerned. If men were sheep, and if God
would follow the pattern of the Eastern Shepherd, many of us
would not be kept very long in His flock, but sold to the market
for meat. Sheep are kept and cared for by the shepherd so that
they might be productive—and well-kept sheep are productive.
Your spiritual productivity, or the lack of it, reveals to you and
to the world your right relationship with Christ, the Good Shepherd. Jesus once said that you can recognize a follower of His—
a Christian from a non-Christian—by the fruit he bears. The
meaning of this is quite simple: "cared-for" sheep, because of
their care, are always better producers of wool than wild sheep.
The fleece of "cared-for" sheep speaks well for its shepherd; it
reveals the care given by the shepherd. One cannot live within
the sheepfold of the Good Shepherd and not be a producer of
wool. God is not interested in the name of the church that carries your name on its roll here on earth; He looks at the wool on
the back of the sheep—so does the world.

"Thou anointest my head with oil; my cup runneth over."
Let us turn back again to the story with which we started this
message. When the man found himself trapped beneath the
heavy streetcar, in a situation over which he had no control, his
greatest danger was not in a bruised body, but in the shock
suffered from the accident. It was discovered that, during the
early bombings of London, more people were dying from shock
than shell fragments. Man was not made to walk alone—he cannot walk alone through life's reverses successfully. The unknown

man who crawled beneath the streetcar and put his arms around the injured man was able to calm a man who was on the verge of being destroyed by shock. In sharing himself with the man, he saved the man.

Christ came to earth to share Himself with man. He shared himself, first, with the human race by becoming a part of it. Christ, very God, took on the form of man. But He did not stop there. He shared the nature of man by accepting the sins of the human race upon Himself as he died on the Cross of Calvary. Nor did He stop there, for He is sharing Himself with all those who accept Him into their lives—He shares Himself in every circumstance of this life and shall do so out in the unknown ages that lay ahead of every human being. Man cannot share the Spirit of God and not have the Spirit do something to his own spirit. It is this transformation that makes the sheep of God different from the wild sheep of the world. "Cared-for" sheep are better than wild sheep.

One of the striking statements made about the early followers of Christ was made by some pagans of that day when "They took note that they had been with Jesus." Something of Jesus had been absorbed into their nature so strongly that it was reflected out of the lives of the followers of Jesus to such a degree that they were marked as the "men who had been with Jesus." And let me hasten to say, this mark was not one of so-called "cloth of the church." The difference was in their personalities. "Cared-for" sheep are better than wild sheep. Does such a difference show in your own life today?

Myself

One day I looked at myself,
At the self Christ can see;
I saw the person I am today
And the one I ought to be.

I saw how little I really pray,
  How little I really do;
I saw the influence of my life—
  How little of it was true.
I saw the bundle of faults and fears
  I ought to lay on the shelf;
I had given a little bit to God;
  But I hadn't given myself.
I came from seeing myself,
  With my mind made up to be
The sort of person Christ can use
  With a heart He may always see.

CHAPTER 22

It Is Unhealthy to Be Unhappy

In chapter 20, we saw expressed in this Twenty-Third Psalm God's desire for all his children to be happy while living on this earth. He made the world so that He, God, could make his children happy. We also noted that unhappiness on this earth does not mean that we are to be happier in heaven, nor is it a sin for one to be happy—supremely happy—in this life. The author of the Twenty-Third Psalm expressed it this way, "Surely goodness and mercy shall follow me all the days of my life."

David had learned, as a shepherd, that happy, contented sheep were, as a general rule, healthy sheep. Healthy sheep lived longer and produced better wool. It was part of the shepherd's duty, not only to see that his sheep had the best pasture and the coolest water, but he also had to protect his sheep from being discontented. The Carnation Milk Company has a slogan which says, "milk from contented cows." This is backed up by a picture of healthy, fat cows grazing in a pasture of deep grass, suggesting to us that milk from such cows, contented cows, is better milk.

One of the outstanding marks of the life of Christ while He was on earth (and the same was true of the early Christians) was the mark of happy living. Jesus said of His mission that He came to give men abundant life. The happy Christian is the most productive of all Christians. The depressed, the despondant, the gloom-scatterer, does much harm to God's kingdom. Christ wants all His children to be happy—happy here on this earth.

Now, since God wants all of us to be happy and has made this world so that He could make us happy, whence comes all the unhappiness we see in the lives of so many so-called Christians? An honest examination of our lives will reveal that we create most of our own unhappiness, either by direct or indirect action. "Goodness and mercy shall follow me all the days of my life." This is true, but we will not tarry long enough on life's road to let it catch up with us. Let us look at three things, three truths, which ought to help us see and understand ourselves better as we seek out the illusive thing we call "happiness."

It has been the observation of many that the Christians of this world who have been dealt the hardest blows from life seem to be the happiest people in our churches. Just pause for a second or two and review a few happy faces you have known. Is this not true of them? One of the sweetest and finest Christians I have ever known lived under hardships that would have broken most of us. She found strength in her faith in God to use these hardships to sweeten her life, and to add spiritual radiance to her personality.

If we could not control our attitudes within ourselves, we would not find any happy people among the burdened, the handicapped, and the millions who have to fight for life itself. I have seen a child get more happiness out of a rag doll not worth twenty-five cents than some people get out of a Cadillac convertible.

My wife and I were married in September, the start of my second year in Seminary. We did not have a G.I. Bill to see us through, and things were pretty tough not only on us, but all the married students, for it was in the middle of the Great Depression. That Christmas, our first together, a Sunday School class of a wealthy church, with more pity, I am afraid, than love for us, brought to each of these married couples a Christmas basket, and as they left one apartment, one of them expressed an opinion of pity for the "poor, struggling, preacher students and their poor wives." We were very poor, that was true of every one of us, but we did not know it then. We were so full of happiness, love for each other, and eagerness for an education, we did not have time to feel sorry for ourselves. There was more happiness on that campus per square inch than anywhere in the world. Incidentally, we thanked the ladies for our basket, then found someone on campus with less than we had, and we gave it to them.

Happiness is grounded within our own heart. It grows from within and moves outward; it does not start outward and come in. The Christian ought to be happy because of what he has within —the love and the spirit of God. During the Civil War days, an old Negro woman was trying to console her white mistress who was depressed and sick. Her mistress said to the ole Mammy, "Mammy, I never see you unhappy or depressed no matter how bad things get around you. What is the secret of your happiness?" The old Negro servant replied, "When I see the black clouds come rolling in on me and it appears these black clouds will settle down on me, crushing me, I just whips around on the other side of them and I finds Jesus there—the bright side is always where Jesus is." Jesus said, "My peace I give unto you." This peace is to and for all those who will claim it for themselves.

If a Christian is not happy, it might be that he has forsaken the security of the flock. The unhappy church members I know do not attend church very often. Their unhappiness is not the result of being mistreated by their church, though often they make such a claim, but their unhappiness stems from their forsaking of the flock—their duties and responsibilities within their own church. There is not a single promise in the Bible or a promise of a blessing for anyone of God's children who tries to serve him outside of his flock.

When a sheep leaves the shepherd's flock, he goes out into the wilderness without the daily care of the shepherd. He cannot share in the daily inspection of the sheep—the daily anointing of his bruises and cuts, nor the refreshing drink from the shepherd's cup at night. He is out in the wilderness to fight his own battles—battles he cannot win. He is at the mercy of the wild animals. He cannot match their skills, nor can he escape from their fangs when he is trapped.

The tragedy of the unhappy Christian is in the fact that he, himself, is not aware of his danger. He does not realize that he is the greater loser. It is true that his wool will be missed, but a shepherd always replaces each lost sheep—so will God. The sheep loses its life in the end. The wandering, professed Christian—if he is really a Christian—can find no peace and happiness living outside of the church of God. Our church can get along without our presence, but we cannot get along very well without our church. We need its inspiration, fellowship, and guidance.

Jesus once said, "Blessed, or happy, is that one who is persecuted for my name's sake." The key to happiness is found in the words "name's sake." The Christian who is living for Christ can never be made unhappy, regardless of the problems he faces, for Christ says that He will fill such a life with "His peace," "His happiness."

One of my friends of long standing has never been a very happy nor a very productive Christian. He is a man of many talents and with great potential—talents never used with much success, and potential never fully realized. He is one of those persons born in the objective mood. He has spent much of his time finding fault with the programs of his church, its lay leadership, and also its leadership from the pulpit. No business meeting is ever held in his church without his sounding off about something. Every "t" must be crossed, and every "i" must be dotted according to the rules of order. He flits from church to church with his membership. He stays three or four years with each church. He is now making a second round of the churches in his city. Whenever I see him, I inquire first where he is now holding church membership, then I have to listen to him as he points out all the things that need to be corrected in that church. He has been a wonderful friend to me, but I am so grateful that he has never been in a position to become a member of any church I have served as pastor. What is wrong with this man? He is one of those sheep who does not like to feed with the flock. He wants to eat on the fringes of his church. He has set himself up as a keeper of the flock, without the qualifications of a shepherd. He has been a very unhappy Christian for many years. Actually, there is nothing really wrong with the churches to which he has belonged. Thousands of others belong to these churches and live within them in peace and happiness. I know that he thinks that most church members do not measure up to his mental ability, or else they would be as unhappy as he is. But what he does not know, and I have been unable to show him, is that his trouble is all within his own heart. I have known, and know, a lot of church members just like this man. You cannot be a happy Christian and live outside of the flock of God. I would remind you of this fact; a sheep can graze with the flock and still live outside of it in attitude.

The story of the prodigal son, as told by Jesus, could be called the story not of "the prodigal son," but of "the two prodigal sons." The elder brother did not leave home, but stayed home and was just as much a prodigal as his younger brother. For he was one in his mind. He did not rejoice when his brother returned. He was the only one in the entire household to voice a protest over the return of his brother, and he was the one who stormed at his father for not appreciating his remaining with the father while the other brother was out in the world having a good time. Of the two sons, the younger displayed the better attitude toward his father and brother. There can be no happiness in the service of Christ for a professed Christian if that one lives in the negative mood, and forsakes the responsibilities of his church. In forsaking his responsibilities, he loses the joy he ought to have in Christ. He pays for this neglect of his church in personal discontent and unhappiness. He loses the "goodness and mercy" that should follow him all the days of his life.

A third fact that can be said about unhappy church members

is that they are unhappy because they are trying to live against God's spiritual laws. Nature teaches the members of its kingdom that each member must conform to the laws of nature to be happy or normal in growth. For example, nature provides for each plant a moisture requirement for its growth and health. If some plants are submerged in too much water, they die. Their nature or law of their nature has been violated. Nature destroys all things that try to live against its fixed laws. If you jump off a tall building, the law of gravity will kill you.

Someone has said that all visible things have a wrong and a right handle. He who takes anything by its wrong handle finds them destructive and harmful, but when one takes them by the right handle, he finds them good and helpful. Take a knife for an example. Take it by its wrong handle, or end, and you will get cut. Take it by its right end, and it will cut for you. Take a match by its wrong end, and it will burn your hand, but take it by its right end, and it will kindle your fire, light your pipe, and serve you helpfully in some way.

God's grace has two handles—two sides to it. Take the grace of God into your life and use it rightly and it is a divine blessing. It is through the Grace of God that comes to men from Christ that gives us life and sustains our lives. If we use this grace daily, we grow spiritually greater each day. Reject this grace, or fail to use it, and it works against you. It will make you a contented and happy Christian; the lack of it, on the other hand, will make you miserable. It will enrich your life; the lack of it, will fill your life with spiritual poverty. You alone can determine which of the two things grace will do for you.

Jesus once said in the Gospel of Luke 11:23, "He that is not with me is against me; he that gathereth not with me, scattereth." Not to live for Christ is to live against Christ. Not to stand for the things of Christ is to take a stand against the things of Christ. There can be no middle ground in respect to the things of the spirit. Not to accept and use the grace of God is abuse of this grace. No one can do this without a spiritual penalty being assessed against him. Man makes his own choices—each professed Christian makes his own daily choices. Unhappiness in the life of a Christian comes as a direct result of living out of the will or against the will of God for your life. You can blame no one except yourself. No one can make you unhappy if you refuse to be unhappy. "Surely goodness and mercy shall follow me all the days of my life." But man must be willing to accept and use this offered mercy and goodness of God, if he would have the earthly happiness God wants all of His children to have.

The Goal

I care not that the storm sways all the trees,
    And floods the plain and blinds my trusting sight;
I only care that o'er the land and seas
    Comes somewhere Love's perpetual peace and light.

I care not that sharp thorns grow thick below,
    And wound my hands and scar my anxious feet;
I only care to know God's roses grow,
    And I may somewhere find their odor sweet.

I care not if they be not white, but red,
    Red as the blood drops from a wounded heart;
I only care to ease my aching head
    With faith that somewhere God hath done His part.

I care not if, in years of such despair
    I reach in vain and seize no purpose vast;
I only care that I sometime, somewhere
    May find a meaning, shining at the last.
           —FRANK W. GUNSAULUS, *1856-1921*

CHAPTER 23

Death with Dignity—
the Glories of Death

One of my golfing partners, not long ago, was complaining about the poor air service between Mobile and another Southern city. He said, "When I fly up to Atlanta on business, I have to remain overnight for there is no evening plane back to Mobile. The older I get, the more my home means to me. I have had my share of hotel rooms and travel during the years, and when night comes, I want to be home with my family." I believe that the older we all get, the more we feel as this businessman feels. As the years come and go, and the older we get, the more our minds turn toward the things of the other world. It is quite a shock to anyone when he stops to consider the short span of years ahead of him. There is a time in life when we cannot project ourselves into any plan on this earth beyond a certain number of years. If you are fifty, and live the normal years of an average American, you ought not to plan beyond the next sixteen years, for chances are, you will not be around to carry through any plans beyond that date. Sickness, accidents, and wars cut many of us down before we live the average span of life.

Death would be a horrible thing to face in our future if we had no hope, no assurance of life beyond the grave. It would be even more disturbing if we knew that we would live beyond the grave—live in hell, in eternal punishment. All the pleasures of life would become bitter ashes to us. Life would be like the last meal offered to a man condemned to die. He can have his choice of anything he wants to eat—perhaps this is the first time in his

183

life he could have anything and everything he wanted to eat—but food has little attraction to a person who is to die in a few hours.

I read recently, with a great deal of interest, an article written by a famous athlete describing his experiences when he was seized with a heart attack. He said he did a lot of soul-searching during the many weeks in bed and the two years he spent trying to regain his health, but he said it was a rich experience, and that he was now getting more from life than before because he had found a quietness of soul—soul peace in this experience. No longer did money have the attraction it once had.

When the question of eternity has been settled in your life, the present life on this earth will have more meaning for you, and you will get more from it. Man can settle this eternity question in this life—and he ought to. Repeat again the last line of this Twenty-Third Psalm: "And I will dwell in the house of the Lord, forever." What a golden nugget with which to close out this wonderful Psalm, and also to close out our study of it in this Twenty-Third message. "Surely goodness and mercy shall follow me all the days of my life, and I shall dwell in the house of the Lord, forever." Let me suggest three things to you from this text.

First, ownership carries with it responsibilities toward that which is owned. Sheep belong to the shepherd. They are his by possession. He knows them by name. He has provided for them all the days of their lives. They are not sold for mutton in the markets, but are loved and protected by the shepherd. The death of one sheep is a personal loss to the shepherd. The Christian belongs to the Good Shepherd. We are His possessions. His responsibility to us is not ended, nor is our relationship terminated, at death. This is an important fact for us to know. Not only do we possess God through faith, but He possesses us. We are his by ownership. One does not become a piece of driftwood on the sea of death, tossed to and fro by the whims of the winds or by the tides of eternity; we are like ships with a pilot aboard to guide us safely into the eternal harbor of God. The souls he guides through the dark waters of death are too precious to let another pilot them. Jesus said, "Lo, I am with you always, even unto the end of the ages."

Jesus said a very wonderful thing in one of his prayers. He was praying for his own. He first defined these as the ones who accepted his teachings about himself—those who had accepted him as the Son of God, or the promised Messiah, and then he said this: "I pray not for the world, but for them that Thou has given me; for they are thine . . . I have kept them." Do not let anyone tell you that you do not belong to God. You should never say, "I hope I am one of His children." Do not try to live through a life so fraught with dangers and uncertainties without the full assurance that you can—that you do—belong to God; that you are His possession—a prized and precious one at that. Jesus, himself, said that you belong to God.

We are possessed by God, and God possesses eternity, so the Christian has nothing to fear from eternity. God had made eternity for us to possess. Jesus said just before he returned to be with the Father, "I go away to prepare a place for you." And then he said, "I will return again." Why? "To receive you unto myself, that where I am you may be also." "And I shall dwell in the house of the Lord forever."

I confess to you that I do not know a great deal about the things after death. One ought not to be disturbed by those who claim to know a great deal about this subject, for no man knows much about heaven or hell. I am not getting very excited about the many prophecies about the dateline for the end of the world. So much that we hear is just another man's speculation—and that is all. One thing is very plain, because it came from the lips of Jesus. Man is not to waste time trying to figure out God's eternal schedule of final events, for He said plainly that no man knows the hour or the day. We are told that we are to work, expecting

Christ to return at any time. I know that Christ is to return, and that satisfies my heart about the question of when!

I might not know a great deal about life after death, for little is said about this subject in the Bible, but I do know a great deal about the God of Eternity and the Saviour of Eternity, and I know that they can be trusted with the things I do not know. It was Paul the Apostle who said, "I know whom I have believed and am persuaded that He is able to keep that which I have committed unto Him against that day." I get great satisfaction out of the fact that I belong to God and that I am possessed of Him. David was speaking from a personal experience with his God and not doing some wishful thinking when he wrote, "Surely goodness and mercy shall follow me all the days of my life, and I shall dwell in the house of the Lord forever." It will be this fact that will make the last few seconds spent on this earth peaceful ones for the Christian—we will be going out of an alien world into our rightful possession. God is simply claiming His own to be with Him in person.

David began this great Psalm with the words, "The Lord is my shepherd, I shall not want," and there can be but one natural ending for it, "and I shall dwell in the house of the Lord forever." We are possessions of our God.

A second fact cannot be ignored. If God cares for His sheep here on this earth, and this is the theme of this Psalm, will God desert or forsake his sheep at death—at the time man needs his God most? "Surely goodness and mercy shall follow me all the days of my life." Good, wonderful—but do not stop there, God, for ahead of every man are the clouds of death. But the shepherd did not stop there; he did not end his sentence there with a period. He could not, for it is the real beginning for man. "And I shall dwell in the House of the Lord forever." This is the goal of every life—to live forever in peace and harmony with God.

Would a mother or a father give their children the best of themselves when the sky is clear and then forsake their children at the first sign of a storm? Does the love of a parent end when the child dies? Would a good parent forsake a child at the first sign of a disease? Of course not. Neither would God share His goodness and mercy with us during this life and then slam the doors of eternity in our faces at death. David did not know as much about eternity as the average Sunday School pupil knows today, but he knew the nature and character of his God. If God did not let him down in this life, God would not let him down after death. If God could be trusted with the things of this life, He can be trusted with the things of the next life. Would God be less consistent than man? Faith is not blind acceptance of some things we wish to obtain. Faith is anchored in the experiences of the past. God does not demand blind faith of anyone. He reveals enough of Himself to all men to lead them into the security of an anchored faith. If you can trust God with your life and your soul while you are upon this earth, surely He can be trusted with your life and soul after death. "And I shall dwell in the house of the Lord forever."

This last fact—the glory of all glories, sweetest of all the sweet, the most beautiful of all things beautiful, and the most thrilling of all human thrills—Heaven is a place, "and I shall dwell [not exist] in the house [not a theory of a ghostly place] of the Lord forever." Hell shall be a physical place, and so will Heaven be a physical place. Heaven will not be a place of golden streets and pearly gates. So often we get caught up in our own figures of speech that we lose touch with reality. The picture, in Revelations, of the city of golden streets is not Heaven, itself, but only one city of Heaven, the New Jerusalem, the capital city, the City of God. We have pictured elsewhere in the Bible men sitting under their own fig trees; pictures of rivers, of trees, and of fruit. The Bible also speaks of a New Heaven and a New Earth. Heaven will encompass both this earth (made anew) and the upper regions we call Heaven. It will be a physical habitation for the physical bodies of the redeemed.

Frankly, Heaven would not seem very attractive to me if I had to think in terms of myself as a sort of ghost floating around in empty space, as I heard one teacher describe life after death. Such spirits would have no need for a physical place. If this is to be the type of home we are to have, Jesus is wasting His time now building for his children the "many houses" he is having prepared for his own. He said, "I go to prepare a place for you, and if I go to prepare a place for you, I will come again to receive you unto myself, that where I am, there you may be also." Jesus has been busy about this task for some two thousand years —not spinning cobwebs out of his imagination for human ghosts or spirits, but preparing a place more wonderful than human eyes have ever seen on this side of Heaven. My mother and dad, both of whom have gone to be with the Good Shepherd years ago, will be there, and I expect to see them in a glorified human form, like unto the body Jesus had after his resurrection. This is not fiction, but fact—"and I shall dwell in the house of the Lord forever."

One cannot read the history of the human race, made up of war, famine, suffering, hardships, and human misery without saying, "There ought to be a place somewhere, where men might escape from such things. And if there is no such place, man is little better off than the other animals of the world." When one faces the injustices of this world, justice cries out for a place for justice, and vindication for all the injustices man suffers. If there were no such place as Heaven, man would be a fool to be honest, sacrificial in his services to others, or even to members of his own family. The thief and the murderer would be right to get what they wanted regardless of whom they harm or destroy. When one sees a loved one suffering from some terrible disease, your sense of justice cries out for a place where there is no suffering, no tears, no pain. Heaven is this place. It is a physical home of beauty and perfection, created by God the Father for all His children. Here they will find fulfilled all the unrealized longings of the heart and the hunger of the soul for complete peace.

Why should God's children be afraid of death when it is the only entrance into immortality? Why should we shed hopeless tears for some loved one who has preceded us into the glories of Heaven? Would we want to hold them back, to again tread the human treadmill of suffering, when their feet can walk the stardust streets of Heaven? Would we want them to again have their eyes reddened by human tears after Christ had wiped their eyes free from all tears? No, I do not believe that anyone would be that selfish. So why fear death when we know "we shall dwell in the house of the Lord forever."

We close this book with the prayer that you have found some measure of comfort in these pages, and have had your faith in the Lord strengthened. Read this Psalm often, especially when you are discouraged or surrounded with fears. Read it slowly and thoughtfully . . .

"The Lord is my shepherd; I shall not want. He maketh me to lie down in green pastures. He leadeth me beside the still waters. He restoreth my soul. He leadeth me in the paths of righteousness for his name's sake. Yea, though I walk through the valley of the shadow of death, I will fear no evil; for Thou art with me. Thy rod and Thy staff they comfort me. Thou preparest a table before me in the presence of mine enemies; Thou anointest my head with oil; my cup runneth over. Surely, goodness and mercy shall follow me all the days of my life and I shall dwell in the house of the Lord forever."

A famous English actor was once asked to give a reading at a private party, and when he had finished, a retired minister, thrilled by the actor's ability to read, asked him to read the Twenty-Third Psalm. He promised to do so with the understanding that the minister would also read it. The actor held his audience spellbound with his perfect tones, his shading of words, his gestures and emphasis on the right words. When he finished reading the Psalm, the crowd burst into applause. The old minister stood and began to read the Psalm again. His voice did not have the silvery tones of the actor, nor did he have the ability to shade words with the proper emphasis, and when he had finished, no applause greeted him. As he sat down, only a holy hush was felt by all. The actor, visibly moved, stood and broke the silence as he said in a voice filled with emotion, "I stirred your minds with my ability to read. He stirred your souls with the words that he read. I know the Psalm, but he knows the Shepherd of the Psalm."

"The Lord is my Shepherd." Is He your Shepherd?

Epilogue

"He leadeth me in the paths of righteousness *for His name's sake*." What's in a name? "The shepherd and his flock" is not merely a poetical figure of speech in the Bible. It was a most familiar object from Mount Carmel to Mount Gilead, from Mount Hermon to the pastures of the wilderness of Paran, and the green hills were covered with flocks of sheep and their shepherds.

In the quotation above, we find two challenges and a choice with which we close this book. "He leadeth me in the paths of righteousness for His name's sake," is not a religious platitude or a pious gesture for others to hear or see. Sheep have no spiritual concepts—not even toward their shepherd. They respond to the shepherd because of learned conditioned reflexes. The shepherd is followed by his sheep without question or rebellion because past experiences with this shepherd have conditioned the sheep to trust his leadership. God challenges us to trust Him and obey Him on His past performances. God is not requiring us to act on "blind faith." Just the contrary. God says, "Test me, try me," then act "for His name's sake." God puts His name on the line for us.

"Paths of righteousness" have nothing to do with spiritual exposure, nor spiritual experience. It is not based upon a religious code of ethics that become "right" because God declared them right, or perhaps because some person in a position of greater respectability than others may have declared them to be right.

When God gave to Moses the Ten Commandments, those Ten Commandments did not suddenly become sacred laws to be obeyed because God gave utterance to them. God gave these laws to man because He knew that they were good and right for man. God knew that man, living under these Commandments, could live a better life and a more profitable life in all areas of society—physical, spiritual, social, and moral. This is also true of the teachings of Jesus. This sacred challenge is to test this sacred truth and prove its validity for ourselves.

191

"For His name's sake." God is saying that He has put His name—His Holy Name—on the line. The redeemed honor His name. A successfully lived life honors the Name of God. God is challenging us to consider what God has invested in the "Paths of righteousness" for us to travel on.

The choice is clear. The Bible says that two roads were offered to men. Life is traveling one of these two roads. The choice is ours—not God's. Each road offers a new day of unknowns. Each road leads to a different destination. The exit of each is the same—death. Would it not be prudent and wise to choose the one prepared for us by God?

What's in a name? If man turns to God's way—for God's name's sake—there can, and will, be peace.

> How sweet the name of Jesus sounds in a believer's ears!
> It soothes his sorrows, heals his wounds, and drives away his
>   fears,
> And drives away his fears.
>
> It makes the wounded spirit whole, and calms the troubled
>   breast;
> 'Tis manna to the hungry soul, and to the weary, rest,
> And to the weary rest.
>
> Dear name! The rock on which I build my shield and hiding
>   place;
> My never failing treasure, filled with boundless stores of
>   grace!
> With boundless stores of grace.
>
> Jesus, my shepherd, brother, friend, my prophet, priest, and
>   king,
> My Lord, my life, my way, my end, accept the praise I
>   bring,
> Accept the praise I bring.
>
> —JOHN NEWTON, 1725-1807